The Author

Glen Hale Bump spent 30 years in advertising and public relations before taking early retirement at the age of 54. His business travels took him all over the United States as well as to Mexico, Canada, and Europe.

Glen Bump and his wife Frances live in Orlando, Fla. They have two sons: Richard, who teaches at Hampden DuBose Academy, Zellwood, Fla.; and David, a ministerial student at Southeastern Baptist Seminary, Wake Forest, N.C. Bump is a deacon of Southside Baptist Church in Orlando, whose pastor, the Rev. Luke B. King, Jr., describes him as "one of the finest Christian men I have ever known."

how to SUCCEED in BUSINESS without being a PAGAN

Glen Hale Bump

While this book is designed for the reader's personal use, it is also intended for group study. A leader's guide is available from your bookstore or from the publisher at 95¢.

Published by

VICTOR BOOKS

a division of SP Publications, Inc.
WHEATON, ILLINOIS 60187

Second printing, 1975

Library of Congress Catalog Card No. 74-77451
ISBN 0-88207-712-0

VICTOR BOOKS
A division of SP Publications, Inc.
Box 1825 • Wheaton, Ill. 60187

To God, who created me,
Christ, who saved me, and
family and friends, who
encouraged me, this book
is dedicated.

CONTENTS

Foreword

A person who wants to succeed in business—or, for that matter, in any endeavor—is bound to come up with some hard questions to answer. He may get the impression that if he conforms to Christian principles he will have to sacrifice some business success. He will read or hear about some who have made a great success and have not hesitated to cut corners and do questionable things. He will need to decide whether he's going to follow that route or hold firm to principles that he has been taught—and that he believes in, if he's a Christian. This book brings out in an excellent way the questions a person faces, and points out answers he can apply to his own life.

Reading is most important for the person who wants to succeed. The ideas of other successful people are available and ready for use. But more important than any other reading is the Bible itself. That is God's Word, and it is a treasure house for the Christian. Make it a firm habit to read some portion of Scripture every day, and it will make your life more successful regardless of your activity.

God does not promise success as such, or wealth as such, even if a person does strictly conform to right principles. Success and wealth can be dangerous, leading a person astray and preventing his full spiritual development. Furthermore, God needs people in every walk of life and at every level of society. He has given people different types of abilities to fit into the areas in which He wants them.

While God does not promise business success to everyone, I agree wholeheartedly with the author that living up to one's convictions and principles on the basis of integrity and faith in God will not stand in the way of a successful business career in a field that God wants you to be in. This book gives many examples. I know of many others from my personal experience.

As a matter of fact, I believe that a person who lives up to sound principles develops better character, one of the most important factors in success in any area. There will be temptations and there will be hard decisions to make from time to time, and these will test a person's character.

Stay true to what God tells you, even though at times it may seem you're making a sacrifice. In the long run, you'll be better off. This is not the route to popularity, but you will gain the respect of others as well as self-respect, and this is far more important than popularity. As you read this book, you will get the answers to many question that you'll face, or have faced, and, hopefully, you will determine you're going to stand true to God.

W. Maxey Jarman
Chairman (ret.), GENESCO

1
You Don't Have to Conform

Success! Whether measured in money, prestige, a sense of accomplishment, or in other terms, it's sought by persons in every size company—from the one-man operation to the multi-national corporation. Whether you're salesman or accountant or junior executive—or vice president with your own carpeted office, private secretary, and use of the company plane—success is your goal. If you are already a success, you want to continue to be one.

But sometimes the price is too high. Many are asking, "Must I give my *soul?*" The power of big business, the stories that come from the executive suite, the rapid "jet set" life-style, the growing divorce and heart attack rate, and other pressures turn off many people to the opportunities in business.

They want to make the most of their God-given talents and hard-earned education, but are wondering if it's really worth the price they'll have to pay.

The worldly person may look at the "rat race" and say, "Forget it, man. I'm doing my own thing." He may try to withdraw from society by joining a commune. Or he may just quietly drop out, settling for a life that doesn't cost too much.

The vibrant, healthy, normal, positive-minded Christian, however, doesn't want that. He believes in being a responsible citizen, serving his Saviour in the mainstream of activity where he can win others to Christ, earn a good living for his family, and contribute to the church and the support of missionaries spreading the Gospel around the world. He believes there must be a profitable and worthwhile place for him in the business world. Yet he sometimes wonders if he can succeed *without compromising his Christian principles.*

Why not? You *can* succeed in business without being a pagan! I did, and if you will look around, you will find others who are doing so too. I have known Christians in insurance, law, the door-to-door brush business, industrial editing, military service, publishing, railroading, banking, and air-conditioning, to name only a few. Ohio or Alabama, Australia or Singapore, it doesn't matter. You can succeed, *and* be true to Christ.

My own 30-year career covered selling, sales promotion, advertising and public relations—fields generally considered to be as incompatible with Christian conduct and character as any. Yet I found success without ulcers, scandal, or personal tragedy, because by God's grace I held fast to Christ, daily reading the Bible, praying for guidance, witnessing on the job, and trying to approach situations with Christian love.

You can, too, in your field.

Pressures to Conform

When I first considered a career, the successful

corporation executive was often portrayed as a chain smoker, big boozer, and a man who knew how to "swing" with his secretary, or when out of town. The men who rose most rapidly seemed to be not only those who worked the longest hours, but who spent still more hours with the boss, "drinking their dinner," having a "few" after dinner, and sometimes going on to an all-night alcohol marathon.

Sound familiar?

One junior executive, inviting his boss to dinner at his home, was more interested in selecting cocktails than in providing the boss' favorite food.

Another said to me once, "You don't drink, do you? To find out what's going on in the company you've gotta drink. Nobody's gonna tell you anything in here. You gotta drink with 'em, loosen 'em up."

A senior executive warned me that I would never succeed unless I consented to setting up meetings which involved cocktail parties.

But all this emphasis on alcohol reflected a simple fear—fear of not being accepted, being fired, or failing to rise rapidly if one didn't conform to what he thought was expected of him in this matter of wining and dining the boss and the clients.

This fear, too, apparently made people join in smutty, off-color talk. There was a desperate competition among the younger business executives to be first to tell the boss the newest obscene story. And when the boss or a client told one, the unwritten law commanded that you guffaw heartily.

Worse than the drinking and dirty language, however, was the greedy dishonesty that also seemed to be a part of "getting ahead." I saw people take unfair advantage of each other: warping facts, stealing materials, and getting overly friendly with other peoples' marriage partners.

I have seen people so caught up with trying to "keep in good" with the boss that they hovered around him constantly, actually afraid to be out of his sight. I have seen too many marriages broken because of a man's enslavement to his job, which demands—he thinks—that he must forever travel, imbibe, work late, do endless special favors for superiors and customers, and completely forget his family.

Men Who Wouldn't Conform

I didn't want to live that way, and I learned it wasn't necessary. Strong encouragement came to me from the lives of eminently successful men.

One of the all-time great salesmen was J. C. Penney, a Christian who built the Golden Rule into his business. His first store was called the Golden Rule store.

R. G. LeTourneau, who pioneered the giant earth-moving machines which revolutionized that industry, lived and testified for God and gave Him 90% of his income. LeTourneau used neither strong drink nor strong language, yet made fortunes, established places of higher learning, and in many other ways enriched the world. Read his book, *Mover of Men and Mountains* (Prentice-Hall, Inc., 1960, 1967, and Moody Press, 1967). If LeTourneau could remain a Christian through his rugged life with mule skinners, iron workers, and other he-man types, you can, too, no matter how rough your business surroundings.

Some other outstanding examples of Christian leaders in the world of business are documented in a dynamic little book called *How to Change Your World in 12 Weeks*. It's the work of a Christian businessman who himself is most successful, Arthur DeMoss, president of National Liberty Life Insurance Company, and David R. Enlow, a writer and editor.

They mention, for example, David Lawrence, the late publisher of *U.S. News and World Report,* who declared that "the destiny of the world is in the hands of those statesmen who can faithfully interpret the commands of the Almighty."

They tell of James L. Kraft, founder of Kraft Foods Company. When asked the recipe for success in building the largest enterprise of its kind in the world from an original capital investment of only $65, Mr. Kraft replied:

"The safest, surest, and swiftest road to victory is prayer, the habit of prayer which was once the familiar, everyday blessing it was intended to be in this nation. Its blessings are as powerful today as ever, if we would utilize them. Personal and family prayer, practiced daily in quietness of spirit, could, I believe, alter the whole world as I know it alters individual lives."

In this connection, DeMoss and Enlow quote the late Roger Babson, a highly respected financial expert. "The greatest undeveloped resource of our country is faith. The greatest unused power is prayer. . . . For a long time it has been considered rather smart to be irreligious. Now people must get back to God. . . . They seem to think there is something about prayer that is not exactly red-blooded or two-fisted. When business worries me, I think of God."

Closer to my own field was Bruce Barton, of Batten, Barton, Durstine, and Osborn, one of the country's top five advertising agencies. He found time, along with his business leadership, to actively proclaim the power of Christ through writing and speaking. Among his works are books about Christ and the Bible, *The Man Nobody Knows* and *The Book Nobody Knows* (Bobbs-Merrill Company).

Nonconformists Needed

In the church I attended at the time I was deciding on an occupation was an advertising executive from a major rubber products company. He explained that there are temptations—and people who yield to them—in any business, but that the advertising business has always seemed to get more than its share of bad publicity about this. He assured me that I could hold to my Christian convictions in advertising as well as anywhere. I did, and God rewarded me. I enjoyed satisfaction and fulfillment as a useful member of well-respected companies, dealing in products and services that help to make the world better. I was able to render service to public as well as private enterprises. Yet I never had to drink, smoke, or engage in questionable business or personal activity.

The Apostle Paul wrote, "Do all things without murmurings and disputings that ye may be blameless and harmless, the sons of God, without rebuke, in the midst of a crooked and perverse nation, among whom ye shine as lights in the world" (Phil. 2:14-15).

In this day of the individualist, being a consecrated Christian is the best way to "do your own thing." It makes you stand out, as the verse says, "as lights in the world." People not only notice you; they *study* you. You will be admired by many non-Christians who desire the courage to take your stand. You will inspire weak Christians to live and speak their convictions. Pray daily for strength and guidance through the tobacco-fogged, alcohol-soaked big business atmosphere of urgent phone calls, conferences, and panics, and God will give you all the success you need.

You will not *always* be a shining Christian example. Like Paul, you may too frequently find yourself saying, "For the good that I would I do not: but the evil which I would not, that I do" (Rom. 7:19). You may lose your temper, make mistakes, fail to be considerate, and otherwise err because you are human. But keep trying to make decisions based on what *Christ* would do! You will do things so courageous they amaze you, as well as others. Like the time I quit because I could not believe in a product I was asked to advertise. It was beer. Alcohol figures in more accidents, marital problems, and homicides than any other outside cause. (I say *outside* because every problem at its root is a *spiritual* problem. "Keep thy heart with all diligence; for out of it are the issues of life" (Prov. 4:23.)

The advertising agency where I was copy chief had as one of its accounts a brewery. My preacher often mentioned in his sermons the evils of alcohol. One Sunday I realized that preacher's finger was pointing at me and God was saying, "There's enough beer in the world. Quit the agency! Now!"

In my heart I answered, "Yes, Lord!"

I didn't want to quit and risk putting my family through financial hardship. Nor did I want to think about the possibility that I might have to leave my home in Florida. But when the Lord speaks, you had better obey. The next morning I turned to the *help-wanted* ads, and—wham! "Wanted: Imaginative writer for national company with headquarters in Florida."

Now—20 years later—I can still hardly believe all the Lord rewarded me with for obeying Him. That new job started me at a 25% increase in pay and led to much more later on, plus interesting trips for my wife and myself and other fringe benefits I could never have had in the agency.

A Basis for Nonconformity

I know from experience that one can succeed in business without being a pagan. It takes courage, faith, prayer, and a strengthened fellowship, but *these are available*. Seek them out and live by them. Faith, prayer, and Christian fellowship work for anybody. They worked for me, and I'm no special saint. It would be closer to the truth if I said —with Paul—I am chief among sinners (1 Tim. 1:15).

I was raised in what is loosely called "a Christian home." My parents were honest, law-abiding, God-fearing citizens, morally fine, industrious, clean, and pleasant. Our well-kept home was warm with love and generosity. I was encouraged to study, work hard and walk the "straight and narrow." I was also taught the value of a sense of humor and of taking time to enjoy life.

I was encouraged to go to Sunday School and church, and did so, though my parents seldom went. I saw that, though the Christian life is the ideal to follow, many fail to follow it. Mixing religion with business is often thought to be impractical.

We had no daily devotions at home. If my parents prayed, they kept it to themselves. I was never taught that Christianity is a practical power mechanism and guidance system for everyday problems. Even the preaching and teaching in the church I attended did not get this across to me.

But I began to meet Christian business people who made me see that Christianity, used in every situation, is the key to a happy, successful life. Finally, I knew I must let Christ take complete control of my life, that I must die to self and be born again, taking Christ as personal Saviour (John 3:3 and Matt. 16:25). I did, and then began to learn to live as a Christian.

One lesson I learned was to live by faith in God's instructions and promises. This was taught me most vividly by my wife. When we married, she was a much more devoted Christian than I. She had standards I balked at—such as tithing. Give a tenth of your income (before taxes yet!) to the church? Ridiculous! But she had been doing it all her life and had astounding stories of answered prayer, great rewards, and much more. She finally convinced me to try it—and for more than 25 years it has helped keep life rich, exciting, and full of "extras" we never expected. Tithing is for real! Don't be without it!

But I started to tell you how rotten I am. I've never been a dope head, alcoholic, or criminal, but compared with Christ I am rotten—as all persons are when compared with Him. And He is the One by whom we are all to be measured. That's why I say that what He can do for me He can do for you or anybody; I'm as imperfect as anyone.

Do you still feel you have to conform to what "everybody" is doing in order to succeed in business, because your situation is "different"? If you don't conform you don't stay?

OK. I didn't stay where I couldn't do the Lord's will. Maybe you, too, will have to move. But maybe not. Even in the great new job I went to after I left the agency, there was pressure to conform, drink, and do other things below Christ's standards. But I didn't. The company and its products were clean, wholesome, and useful. I thoroughly believed in them; and I could serve my Lord while serving the company, without conforming to carnal customs that many *thought* they must observe.

Let's see *why* you don't have to conform, no matter what happens.

2

Why You Don't Have to Conform

You don't have to conform to pagan customs to succeed in business, because *all business asks of you is*: *Results!*

Business doesn't care much *who* you are, but *what* you are. True, the boss' son has a better chance of getting a job—and, in some cases, holding it—but even family ties and politics fail eventually unless a person can produce!

Why? Because even the *boss* has a boss! The president reports to the board, and the board to the stockholders, and they all demand results! To succeed you must have ability. "Not slothful in business; fervent in spirit" (Rom. 12:11). Neither education, appearance, method, attitude, or intelligence count like *results!* The factory wants production; top management wants sales and profits; and the stockholders want dividends. Never mind how the results are produced; but get *results, not excuses!*

And how do you get results? Every successful man has his own answer, but most of them, in a word, say: "WORK!" Some believe in working fast, some long, some hard, and some smart.

One of the foremost authorities on business management is Peter Drucker, Professor of Management in the Graduate School of Business Administration of New York University. Born and educated in Europe, Drucker has been newspaperman, economist, and management consultant. One of his many books is *The Effective Executive* (Harper & Row, 1966) in which he gives five qualities that seem to mark successful executives:

1. They know where their time goes.
2. They focus on outward contribution, gearing efforts to results rather than to work.
3. They build on strengths—their own and those of their superiors, colleagues, and subordinates.
4. They set priorities and stay with them.
5. They make effective decisions.

Conformed or Informed?

Robert Townsend, a revolutionary in management thought, fired a blast that woke up a lot of dozing minds with his spritely book, *Up the Organization* (Alfred A. Knopf, Inc., New York, 1970). The man who got everyone to "try harder" because of his successful revitalization of the Avis Rent-a-Car company, Townsend also turned losses into profits for American Express (Senior Vice-President and Director); Dun and Bradstreet (Director and Member of Executive Committee); and CRM Communications/Research/Machines (Chairman of Executive Committee).

Here are some of his ideas in condensed form:

"Admit your mistakes openly. My batting average on decisions at Avis was no better than .333.

"The world is divided into: the few who make

good on promises (even if they don't promise much) and the many who don't. Get into Column A. You'll be very valuable wherever you are.

"Like everything else you do—keep your expense account honest. Even if others are cheating openly. Not because you might get caught, but because honesty has to start somewhere.

"Everybody must be judged on his performance, not on looks, manners, personality, or whom he knows or is related to."

Stanley Tippett, traffic manager for some 87 plants of Container Corporation of America, declares, "One of the most important characteristics of Christian businessmen I've met is their abundant energy. They do so much more than others! I'm also impressed by the logical approach and ability to make decisions I've seen in Christian businessmen. They are far from being 'wishy washy.'

"I think in particular of one man who was president of a company. He taught two Sunday School classes, was on several mission boards, taught several Bible classes, and had many speaking engagements. Yet he never appeared tired!

"A third favorable impression is the true humility of some of the very successful businessmen I have met, all great competitors. They have been successful by exercising their talents—not through the road of unusual entertainment or questionable practices. (They also work very hard.)"

DeMoss and Enlow define success as *making the maximum use of one's God-given abilities in the pursuit and progressive attainment of a specific goal in harmony with God's will.*

To do this they tell us to:

take inventory of our lives

determine to want only the perfect, directive will of God

be flexible, check out every possibility

They quote Lee S. Bickmore, chairman of the board of the National Biscuit Company, who once gave four price tags on success:

painstaking preparations

helping others to grow

high aim

long days and sleepless nights

One absolute essential to success, say DeMoss and Enlow, is receptivity, which includes

ability to accept criticism gracefully

the gift of enlarging one's capacity.

They point out *enthusiasm* as an essential for success, quoting variety store magnate S. S. Kresge at the age of 95: "One of the most important ingredients in a person's makeup for successful business operations is enthusiasm."

Developing the principle further, they give us automobile tycoon Walter Chrysler's view: "Yes, more than enthusiasm, I would say excitement. I like to see men get excited. When they get excited, they make a success of their lives."

The authors refer to Andrew Carnegie, founder of U.S. Steel, as Carnegie champions single-mindedness: "Concentrate your energy, thought, and capital exclusively upon the business in which you are engaged. Put all your eggs in one basket and then watch that basket, day and night."

DeMoss and Enlow reveal what they call their Million Dollar Secret: "Never say a single word of any kind to an associate, employer, employee, neighbor, or member of your own family until first you have assured yourself in your own mind and heart that what you are about to say is to be said in love."

R. G. LeTourneau said, "When I was hiring out for pay, I made it a point of stepping along a little faster and finding ways to do a job a little quicker. . . . By accepting God as your partner, no limit can be placed on what can be achieved. . . . Ever since the birth of our Saviour, the time hasn't been when a good Christian can't work rings around the toughest roughneck you ever saw. . . . You will never improve unless you blame yourself for the troubles you have. Then when you realize your troubles are your own, you can take them to the Lord, and He will give you guidance."

An authority on success in a more secular vein is Napoleon Hill, author of *Think and Grow Rich* (Napoleon Hill, 1937, and The Ralston Publishing Company, Cleveland, Ohio, 1953) an all-time classic in success literature. Hill was chosen by Mr. Carnegie to organize the "Science of Success" based upon Carnegie's lifetime experiences and those of more than 500 other top-ranking business and professional men. These included presidents Woodrow Wilson and Theodore Roosevelt, Thomas A. Edison, Henry Ford, John D. Rockefeller, and Alexander Graham Bell. The 13-point formula points out such proven ingredients of success as:

a burning desire to accomplish one definite goal

belief and faith that you can do it

imagination

organized planning

decision

persistence.

In a later book, *How to Raise Your Own Salary* (1953, Napoleon Hill Associates, A Division of Clement Stone Enterprises, Chicago), Hill says, "We look at the records of such men as Andrew Carnegie, Henry Ford, and Thomas A. Edison . . . and we marvel, not suspecting perhaps, that back of these achievements is a plan far more profound than that of the desire for riches . . . the Creator's plan to urge men onward . . . by . . . exercise of their personal initiative."

Here are just a few of Hill's success maxims:

"You can do it if you believe you can.

"Cooperation and friendship . . . can be had only by first giving them.

"The ability to ask intelligent questions made Socrates the best educated man of his time.

"The most beneficial of all prayers are those we offer as . . . gratitude for the blessings we already have.

"Two kinds of people never get ahead. Those who do *only* that which they are told to do and those who will *not* do what they are told to do.

"Don't ask your employer why you have not been promoted. Ask the person who knows best—yourself.

"The man who says, 'It can't be done' is usually busy trying to keep out of the way of the man who is doing it."

And some of Carnegie's own rules for success were:

definiteness of purpose
faith
going the extra mile
creative vision
self-discipline
organized thinking
learning from defeat
the Golden Rule
cooperate
budget time and money
make health a habit.

Conform or Reform?

William E. Holler, late General Sales Manager of Chevrolet, whose organization of 90,000 people sold more than 22,000,000 vehicles, had some crisp ideas on success. Here are a few from his book, *Sell America Into Jobs* (Motor City Publishing Company, Detroit, 1945):

"Why does one man go up and another of equal ability go down? The successful . . . made full use of his ordinary talents and ability . . . small things . . . and by constant work and study . . . they became a powerful factor in equipping him to be an 'above the average' man.

"Never forget a customer—and never let a customer forget you.

"If there is any single trait that unites all . . . who force their way upward . . . it is this: *They put more into their work than they ever expect to get out of it—*

Pasteur at his microscope long after his eyes were red-rimmed and blood-shot from strain and fatigue.

Curie standing over a pot of pitchblende while freezing winds swept through the hovel in which he worked.

Caruso practicing hour after hour every day for more than 30 years.

Glenn Cunningham, whose legs were burned so badly that doctors doubted whether he could ever walk again, practiced so long and faithfully that he became one of the greatest milers the cinder track has ever known.

Milton, blinded, stringing parallel wires to guide his pen as he wrote the immortal *Paradise Lost*.

"Talent is not enough. Even genius is not enough. It takes the courage to give *everything* _you have to the cause._

"Make yourself useful—be full of usefulness— and you will make yourself!"

So eager is the business world for results that some companies even tolerate serious indiscipline among their people if only they succeed on the job. I have seen bad temper, excessive drinking, gambling, careless driving, tardiness, marital squabbles, mismanagement of personal finances, and other disruptive problems excused merely because the persons involved were effective workers.

As Drucker says, "Whoever tries to place a man or staff an organization to avoid weaknesses will end . . . with mediocrity. . . . Strong people always have strong weaknesses too."

If you were a manager, wouldn't you prefer an employee whose only hangup is "religion" over an employee who is beset by problems of the type mentioned above?

These authorities have told us that results come mostly from work. "Whatsoever thy hand findeth to do, do it with thy might" (Ecc. 9:10). You can be yourself if you will also be a part of the business machine.

"Now there are diversities of gifts, but the same spirit" (1 Cor. 12:4). Paul is talking about gifts of the Holy Spirit, and the diversity of gifts for serving God, but the principle applies to our gifts for serving man in making our living. You are not going to be handicapped by the individuality you show as a Christian. All kinds of persons can succeed. I trained a series of editors to handle a publication. One was a flurry of energy, with much paper-shuffling, many phone calls, and conferences. Another was neat, soft-spoken, methodical, and hardly seemed to be working. But he was! Some of the men were humorous; others serious. Some had irritating habits or strange attitudes. Yet all did the job!

Drucker emphasizes this point in discussing the three leaders who in his experience were the best in human relations: General George C. Marshall, Chief of Staff of the U.S. Army in World War II; Alfred P. Sloan, Jr., head of General Motors for over 30 years, and one of Sloan's senior associates, Nicholas Dreystadt, who built Cadillac into a successful luxury car in the midst of the Depression.

Says Drucker, "These men were as different as men can be: Marshall, the 'professional soldier,' sparse, austere, dedicated, but with great, shy charm; Sloan the 'administrator,' reserved, polite, and very distant; and Dreystadt, warm, bubbling, and superficially a typical German craftsman of the 'Old Heidelberg' tradition. Every one inspired the deep devotion, indeed true affection in all who worked for them."

Businessmen usually agree that the most precious commodity in the world is *time*. The careful conservation of time, however, is just another means of getting results! As continuity director of a radio station, my job consisted of writing the announcements and placing them in a book in proper order so the announcers could read them on schedule. The station manager said, "You don't have to keep regular hours. Just get the job done." Business says as God does, "It is required in stewards, that a man be found faithful" (1 Cor. 4:2).

So, if you are at your best when you are motivated by serving Christ, that's fine with the business world. "Blessed is every one that feareth the Lord; that walketh in His ways. For thou shalt eat the labour of thine hands: happy shalt thou be, and it shall be well with thee" (Ps. 128:1-2).

Do the job, and if other employees criticize you for your Christian principles, the boss will probably tell them, "OK. He's a religious nut. But he's a great producer! Maybe the *rest* of you should try Christianity!"

You don't have to be old or experienced to succeed in business. Let your individuality shine out, even though you may be criticized. "Better is a poor and wise child than an old and foolish king, who will no more be admonished!" (Ecc. 4:13) "Young Turks" or "Young Tigers" are always welcome in business if they have ability, regardless of how unorthodox their methods or personalities. They are good for the company because:

   they produce results

   they stimulate others to increase their efforts

   their new methods may be adopted as standard
      procedures.

Conformed or Transformed?

Jesus did not conform. He was an innovator. Columbus did not conform. He, too, "changed the shape of the world." Henry Ford did not conform. He *transformed* the automobile from rich man's toy to every man's transportation! You don't need to be an "average" person in business—one who "goes along with the crowd," in drinking, smoking, off-color story-telling, company politicking or whatever is considered regular behavior where you are. You can be your Christian self, serving Christ in your daily conduct, attitudes, and achievements. Just get the job done!

Attending worship twice on Sunday and prayer meeting during the week, and missing a lot of TV shows everyone talks about will not handicap you. Being unable to discuss horse or dog racing or jai alai will not keep you from being promoted if you *earn* a promotion. If, when others order cocktails, you order a "horse's neck" (ginger ale and lemon) or refuse any kind of drink, you will not be laughed out of the company. Container Corporation's Stanley Tippett says, "I refer to myself as the 'ginger ale kid.' I laugh with them. Many people have told me privately they admire my stand, and the easy way it's taken."

It's a free country, and one thing that has built it is pride in individual choice. We work, play, worship, and vote as we please. This democracy of the individual is respected in business. You don't have to conform except in the essentials of the business, and these have nothing to do with religion, politics, relatives, choice of neckties, or automobile.

To the world you are your own person, even though you are really *Christ's!* The world will let you handle the job your way. When asked why I don't drink, I simply answer that it's harmful; it's a bad example; it's against my religion; and, as I have a tendency to overeat, I might also tend to overdrink. So I do not drink at all.

A Christian writer, James C. Hefley, author of *Why Drink?* and many other books, quips when a waitress asks if he wishes a cocktail, "I do not think that I should drink, for if I drink I do not think."

Actually, drinking is one of today's major business problems. Too many people become problem drinkers because they feel they must take a social drink at business functions. You don't have to, though it may seem that the "whole world" drinks. Plenty of executives have learned, the hard way, that they *cannot* drink. So if you refuse, you probably will not be asked why. It will be assumed perhaps that you have a health problem.

As you live a Christian life in business, on the job or off, people will notice that you are "different," but they will respect that difference. Many "average" people long for your spirit of independence. They actually get tired of conforming, but don't have the courage or energy to escape it. Your independent spirit will be refreshing to them. You may be kidded, ridiculed, stared at, or whispered about, but you will also be admired.

Christianity can help you toward success: First, because you are *admired*, and second, because you are *remembered*. You stand out. Some may feel superior to you because they interpret your Christian stand as weakness. Others may feel inferior, or be afraid that your high standards and straight approach to life is a threat to them in the scramble for success. They may not understand your faith. They may feel you have some "angle" because of your friendly, unselfish approach. Some may be wary of you, having been deceived by others who have used a Christian front to mask ulterior motives. Whatever the attitudes you face, your associates will be aware of your presence, and that is an aid to success. Being known helps keep you in a position to be offered new opportunities.

Conform or Perform?

Living a Christian life is not entering a popularity contest. You will not always be loved and followed; but you will be remembered as somebody who *believes in something*. That is a quality much admired in this day of disillusioned, disheartened, and dishonest employees and disgusted management.

Conform? Business doesn't ask you to conform —just to *per*form!

But what if you can't do your best where you are? What if your work seems pitted against your practicing Christianity? Does a "No Christians Wanted" sign light up when you do something the way Christ would? If so, should you stay, try to revolutionize the business, change its policies, show the boss that you know more than he does?

Suppose your Christian conduct gets you fired! Have you misinterpreted the Gospel, become a fanatic, lost touch with reality? Perhaps you should check your personality and your methods. You cannot succeed in life if you are offensive to people on *any* subject, including religion. But you can live your Christian principles in a polite way. You need not retreat to worldly ways and just "go along with the crowd." Never! Your willingness to lose your job for His sake will be one of God's tests for you . . . your Red Sea decision. Moses and the children of Israel did not retreat. They plunged into the water *and it parted*. The two Marys on the way to Christ's tomb wondered how they would roll away the stone, but found it rolled away!

Let's see how other doors can open if your present one shuts.

3
Other Doors Will Open

You have done what you thought right. You have earnestly pursued your career, and suddenly, either by your own doing, or by someone else's, you cannot continue. Either your Christian convictions get you fired, or God says, "This is no place for you. Quit. You cannot serve Me and serve this employer in the way he demands."

This is IT, a turning point. What do you do now? The answer may not come immediately, but you should start to seek it immediately. The first step is to *pray*. Pray for calmness and guidance. This will help you observe the first law of any emergency: *avoid panic*. Praying also enables you to take the next step which is to *think*. Use your imagination, your past experience, your knowledge of the job or business market which interests you. You have received a blow to your ego, your hopes and plans, but you have not lost everything. Your education and past business experience are intact. You still have physical and spiritual health and strength. You are still in touch with God. He still rules the universe He created, and He can handle your little old job problem without the slightest effort.

Next, *talk over the situation* with your marriage partner and perhaps other members of the family; and, if you feel it right to do so, with pastor or other trusted friends. This will help you determine in which direction you should pray further—whether for work in another department of your present firm (if the trouble is just in one area), or for a job in a different company, or perhaps for a complete change to some different occupation. Losing or quitting a job or business has often brought a career of much greater satisfaction and usefulness than the person had before. God says, "I will instruct thee and teach thee in the way which thou shalt go: I will guide thee with Mine eye" (Ps. 32:8). He surely will, for that eye of God can see things when you would declare nothing is there! His vision is not merely 20/20, but Plenty/Plenty!

Next, *have great faith.* You may not have much faith at first, or your faith may start great *and* dwindle if the hunt for a new opportunity goes on and on . . . and *on.* You may need to read a lot of faith passages. Maybe you already have one or two that you turn to automatically when you need a new injection of faith. Mine is Romans 8:31: "If God be for us, who can be against us?" Is that power? What more could you want? Those 10 tremendous words pack a wallop that makes me feel 10 feet tall, springs me up from the floor of discouragement, and sends me back into the fight with the courage of a tiger tamer. I may not get this next job or the next or the next, but God is still ruling the universe, and He is *for* me. If His path lies through trial or hardship, He has a good purpose in that too.

You don't have that much faith yet? Now is the

time to start developing it. And here is where imagination comes in. One of the ways the Bible helps us is by stimulating the imagination. If you're still not ready to use yours, take a big, healthy bite of Hebrews 11, the all-time winner faith chapter. Since we're talking about changing jobs, which may mean that you'll be moving your residence, look first at verse 8: "By faith Abraham, when he was called to go out into a place which he should after receive for an inheritance, obeyed; and he went out, not knowing whither he went."

"Yeah," you may say, "but Abraham was a great patriarch. He was in the Bible. I'm just—"

Abraham had the same God you have. If God could find Abraham in sophisticated Ur of the Chaldees and move him and that flock of relatives and livestock clear across the country without Lyon movers or even U-Haul, He'll have no trouble getting you relocated, not one bit. Imagination, you see? You may want to absorb some more of the convincing faith stories from that chapter or some other places in the Bible.

Faith in Action

Or maybe you're ready now to start putting your faith to work, as J. C. Penney did. In his book, *View from the Ninth Decade* (Thomas Nelson & Sons, New York, 1960), he recounts an experience when, as a young store clerk, he saw his employer cheating customers. When he told his father about it, the elder Penney made him quit the store, even though jobs were scarce. A few years later young Jim remembered his father's command and automatically quit another job when the store owner there wanted him to cheat. J. C. Penney was no quitter when he had an honest job to do, but he had the courage to quit when he knew he could not serve the Lord by staying.

You will need to resist more than dishonesty and immorality, however. There is selfishness, for example, and there is fear. Before the Lord moved me from Akron, Ohio, to Florida, I had a good job for four years with a rubber products company. Weather statisticians say that Akron has about 66 clear days a year. My wife was used to the sunshine of Georgia, where she was born, and Florida, where she spent about half her early years. She wasn't happy in gloomy, sooty Akron.

My natural reaction to her attitude was what most men's would have been: "Tough it out, kid. Akron is where my job is. I'm the breadwinner. Here's where we stay." But I married her for love, and part of Christian love is regard for your marriage partner's wishes.

I began to think about the possibility of returning south, where I had discovered this brown-eyed beauty. I thought even more seriously about it when another problem arose. The doctor told us that our three-year-old, Richard, would be healthier and have a better chance of outgrowing a chronic breathing problem if we got out of the soot and into the sunshine. I began to write to places in the South about job possibilities.

Nothing.

The only way they were going to be interested was if I were living in the South. Hmmm. Move, y'say? Quit this good job with a fine old firm, sell the house, load the family into the car, and head south?

The Lord used a whopping snow and ice storm to help me decide. One night it took me four hours to drive the six miles home from work. Sometimes

God will nudge you a little when your faith wavers. We took a deep breath and made the break. Sold the house and quit the job.

Half of the guys in the office said, "You're nuts."

The other half said, "I wish I had your guts."

That was in 1952, and I haven't shoveled any snow since. Richard and his brother, David, grew up healthy in the sunshine, and we're all living happily ever after. The Lord has provided, and He will provide for you, if you have to change job or location. I had a good deal in Akron, but I often thought as I looked at the grey skies and felt my body throb to the roar of the factory that there were probably more pleasant places to earn a living. The Lord moved me to such places. But he wouldn't have if I had not had the faith to follow His guidance—to leave the place I liked, but my wife didn't, where I could have been happy and successful but my son's health might have suffered. Without exercising that little faith, I would have been something of a pagan. I did exercise it, though, and we have had life more abundantly! If you feel guided to make a change of some kind, have faith, make the change.

The Providence of God

God will provide! Paul says, "But my God shall supply all your need according to His riches in glory by Christ Jesus" (Phil. 4:19). You see, the fact is, He not only *will* supply; He already *has* supplied. Evangelist Manley Beasley brought this strikingly home to me. Here is how he puts it in his *Faith Workbook* (Rev. Manley Beasley, 2318 Fourth Street, Port Neches, Texas 77651, $3): "This is a principle and a law that goes all the way through the Bible. For instance, which came along first? Air for your lungs to breathe or lungs to breathe the air? That is simple. The air for the lungs to breathe." God's provision anticipates our needs.

God had a radio station start in Pensacola, Fla., before He gave my wife and me guidance to move there from Atlanta. This was an earlier faith incident, shortly after we were married, before we ever moved to Akron. Atlanta, where we lived right after World War II, was said to have the second worst housing shortage in the country. The crop of wartime marriages and the lack of house and apartment construction had made places to live almost impossible to find. Because the Naval Air Station in Pensacola was discharging men, however, housing was reportedly available there. We had no car. We had little money. I hitchhiked the 350 miles to Pensacola. Yes, there was housing, and job possibilities seemed good.

I went back to Atlanta, wound up my job, and we moved to Pensacola—on the bus. A tentative job I had lined up at a radio station fell through. But suddenly another radio station opened—the first new station in that town in 25 years! Naturally, preparations for it had been in the works for several months. God's timing is always right. He knew when to get me started for Pensacola. "In all thy ways acknowledge Him, and He shall direct thy paths" (Prov. 3:6).

What we keep forgetting is that God made everything and owns everything and *controls* everything! We keep forgetting how tiny our needs are in comparison with His unlimited supply! God reminds us, "For every beast of the forest is Mine, and the cattle upon a thousand hills" (Ps. 50:10). In less agricultural and more commercial language you could say, "Every automobile on the highway is Mine, and the department stores in a thousand cities." Just because the Bible was written before the Industrial Revolution or the Machine Age, don't think that God doesn't know when you are going to need a new car or open-heart surgery or braces for the kids' teeth. Check the last half of Matthew 6:8: "Your Father knoweth what things ye have need of before ye ask Him."

That includes *everything!* Whether you need a job, house, college education, wife, husband, or child, God can provide it! True, we may not always *need* what we *think* we need. We may only *want* some things God does not want us to have. But if we earnestly live for Him, pray and seek His guidance, He will bless us far more richly than we may think possible, and often in ways we never imagine. Too often we just don't think big enough. We try to limit God. We don't love Him enough to have the faith to believe that He can supply all our *need*—and lots of our *wants* besides!

I could never have foreseen all the good things that would come to my wife, my boys, and myself. We are not wealthy in money, but we have never missed a meal or lacked respectable clothing and housing. We have had illness, accidents, unemployment, and other problems, but they have been more than balanced by happy surprises all along the way.

The more you trust God for, the more He will give you. Manley Beasley, while flying to a series of meetings, was led by the Lord to trust Him for a specific amount of money to come in during the meetings. He actually wrote down the figure and sent it to his wife before the meetings began, as proof of his faith. The amount was a substantial one, more than he would dare to ask, except for his faith.

Once he got a look at the little church where the meetings were to be, his faith wavered. The first frail meeting in the series didn't help a bit. But he trusted in the Lord and wasted no time in worrying. The appearance of the little church and the little congregation was deceiving. Money also came from distant places. The meetings raised every penny of the "unreasonable" amount for which he had been guided to trust God.

Henry Burgess, one of my friends, is a bus driver. He wondered what he was going to do when it was announced that the city bus company was going to shut down. He didn't want to become a long-distance driver and have to be away from home. The Lord provided a job with a local tour line, a better job than he had before.

Another of my friends, Vee Lowe, was told by his firm that he would be transferred out of town. He had recently bought a new home and didn't feel the Lord wanted him to move. The Lord provided. Vee was presented an opportunity to buy a small business. It was a challenge. He had never been in business for himself before. He exercised his faith, however, quit the company which wanted to transfer him, and bought the small business. The Lord has blessed him with success.

Read the lives of LeTourneau, Penney, Kraft, and others who have stood by their Christian convictions and acted with faith. You will see that God always rewards faith . . . and usually with much bigger rewards than expected. As LeTourneau says, "I remember one of my customers who told me, 'I try to shovel out more for God than He can for me, but He always wins. He's got a bigger shovel.' "

But God will shovel more than material blessings. He will give you the spiritual blessings that make all the others worthwhile. He will provide peace, happiness, optimism, and a zest for life that will give you the strength and knowledge to help others. You will grow in self-confidence and in value as a Christian leader.

"Who, me?" you say. "Not me. I'm too weak. I'm —I could never—you just don't know me. I—"

I don't know you, but I know God. And He's got a plan, see? He's helped thousands like you—and thousands worse. All you need at first is the *desire* to have Him help you. You have that or you wouldn't have read this far. So read on.

4

You Are
to Be Special

You have made a brave decision—so brave, in fact, that to many it will seem foolhardy. The first dive from a high board, the first drive in heavy traffic, getting married, take courage. So does initial commitment to Christ—or determining to succeed in business without being a pagan. You have chosen an unconventional course of action, so you are going to have to be unconventionally devoted. You are now a part of what Peter calls "a chosen generation, a royal priesthood, an holy nation, a peculiar people; that ye should shew forth the praises of Him who hath called you out of darkness into His marvelous light" (1 Peter 2:9).

No, you don't have to go into the ministry or any church-related vocation, unless you're guided to do so. You keep right on making top dollar as the best insurance man, 747 pilot, or over-the-road trucker you can be. But notice that part about being a "peculiar" people. It doesn't mean you're going to be an odd-wad holier-than-thou pronouncing hell-fire and brimstone on anyone you see committing some sin, though, if you are the boss you will have to warn such a person to shape up or ship out; and if he doesn't, you will have to fire him.

In what way, then, are you going to be "peculiar"? Greek scholars say the word means "preserved for oneself" or "purchased." As a peculiar or purchased by God person, you are going to attend Sunday School and worship services regularly. I refer you to Hebrews 10:23-25: "Let us hold fast the profession of our faith without wavering; (for He is faithful that promised;) And let us consider one another to provoke unto love and to good works: Not forsaking the assembling of ourselves together, as the manner of some is; but exhorting one another: and so much the more, as ye see the day approaching."

"Wait a minute. Wait a minute! Sunday School? That's for *kids!*"

You, too, Buster. It was no kid, but J. Edgar Hoover who said the Sunday School is the greatest character-building agency in the world. Or doesn't your character need any more building?

Every Sunday?

The average person attends Sunday School and worship when he feels like it. You are going to go week in and week out. Yes, during vacation too. There are churches everywhere unless you're out in the woods—and you can take your Bible and have a little service there, too. Before you go on vacation, leave your tithes and offerings for the Sundays you'll be gone. The preacher likes to get paid as regularly as you do. The people who aren't on vacation like to have the lights, water, and air-conditioning on when you're gone, too. Why church and Sunday School regularly? Because you are on Christ's team and, like any team, it practices regularly. If you're going to play the game, you must practice. Sales organizations have regular sales meetings. Those who don't attend don't stay with the company.

You *work* on Sunday? *Every* Sunday? Sunday *evening,* too? Is your work absolutely essential? Can you not find another job where you don't have to work Sundays? Can the company not replace you with a Jew or a Seventh Day Adventist or Seventh Day Baptist? They worship on another day, so you will not be cutting them out of anything. Think it over . . . think it over a long time. Remember, you're not answering me. You're answering God. You want His blessings and protection, right? You want to succeed in business, right? Then show your faith in God's plan. Go by the Book!

Like a retired service man in our church did. Military men seem to retire young these days—and go right to work somewhere else. Such energy! Joe Smith is a food service man, what civilians call a chef. On one job he had to work Sundays, but he prayed for a job where he wouldn't. The Lord sent him one, and it's a better job than he had before.

Henry, the bus driver, doesn't have to work Sundays. Vee Lowe doesn't work Sundays. Like these men, Joe Smith is a deacon. Is there any pattern here? It has occurred to me that one reason they are all deacons and successful in business is that they have put God first. No, you don't have to be a deacon, elder, or a church officer to succeed in business without being a pagan. But after a time you may find yourself becoming a church leader as a result of living for God on the job. For if you live for Him on the job, you will do so at church.

The principle of remembering the Sabbath Day to keep it holy (Ex. 20:8) has a practical value. Just as you can't go 24 hours every day without rest, neither can you work seven days a week indefinitely. During World War II, war plant workers kept it up for a while, but accidents and product defects increased. You work more efficiently the other six days when you rest and worship on one. I have seen many plans that were made at Sunday extra sessions scrapped on Monday.

Many people I have known who thought they had to work on Sundays are no longer with the companies they served. The busy, busy, oh-so-conscientious, we-never-sleep heroes who blaze away Sunday after Sunday sometimes have other motives besides loyalty, sheer love of what they're doing, or even greed for more money. It can be fear of losing the job or business. Or sometimes they prefer the office, shop, store, or out-of-town trip to their homes. If so, something desperately needs correcting. The family needs to find answers together in God's house. If you're hiding from your family on Sunday, the chances are you're trying to hide from yourself too. And if you're doing that, you're hiding from God. It won't work very long. Adam and Eve found that out. Sooner or later something's going to give—either your happiness or that of someone else or both.

Particularly tragic is the person who actually kills himself with work. God does not intend it to happen. He expelled Adam and Eve from the garden, and put them and everyone else to work, but He didn't say seven days a week.

A thrilling part of the LeTourneau testimony is the story of how he resisted Sunday work at a time when it seemed that if he did not work Sundays he would lose his company. Yet he held firm, and the crisis passed.

Midweek Too?

So much for one day's rest in seven. Now, what about midweek prayer service? I think I heard you mutter, "Zhish! That tears it!" All right, skip it if you travel all the time and have no access to church in the towns where you find yourself on Wednesday or Thursday nights, or are keeping a business appointment at prayer meeting time. By the way, how late do you work on the road? And what towns do you cover that are so small they don't have churches? Not too much business out there, is there?

I know that a traveling person cannot always be regular about prayer meeting. I've traveled. I know that time on the road must be conserved, that planes are late, that hotels and restaurants are crowded, and that you can't always stop and hunt up a church. But have a straight little talk with yourself and see how many times your excuses are legitimate. Start thinking in terms of the possibilities instead of the impossibilities of making prayer meeting a habit—wherever you are.

Here's why: Jesus says, "Watch and pray, that ye enter not into temptation: the spirit indeed is willing, but the flesh is weak" (Matt. 26:41). Where are people tempted most? Isn't it away from home? But regardless, we are all tempted wherever we are by something. That's one reason for the midweek prayer meeting. Who cares who started it? Somewhere along the way somebody realized that the world was crowding in on us too much between Sundays. If we can do as urged in 1 Thessalonians 5:17, "Pray without ceasing," we might not need the midweek prayer service so much, but it is still a good idea because it is a powerful, refreshing experience, actually helping us succeed in the business of living.

How so? First, it lifts our sagging determination. You may go out of church on Sunday ready to revolutionize your business, but by Wednesday or Thursday the chances are you're feeling demolished. But take a prayer meeting pill and you begin to feel a little better. "And He spake a parable unto them to this end, that men ought always to pray, and not to faint" (Luke 18:1). You do feel kinda faint about the middle of the week, don't you? Well, notice the cure: "pray and NOT faint." I have gone into prayer meeting many times ready to toss in the towel. I have almost always come out ready to go some more rounds. What is the strange power in this midweek meeting? The only explanation is the simple one you would give a child, and the one God gives us. By simply talking to God and listening to Him, we are strengthened. We are reminded that we are not alone, in that awful situation that has arisen where we work. God is with us and ready to help.

There's something else at prayer meeting that helps glue you back together: fellowship. And, of course, if you have Bible study there, as many churches do, that, too, is part of the power that gets you moving again. Let's look a little closer at fellowship, though. It helps two ways. First, you may enjoy the first smiles, handshakes, and kind words you've had since Sunday. Second, you get a chance to give out a few yourself. You voice your needs and hear others voice theirs. You may pray for them and they for you. You realize you are among special friends, people who are plugged into a

Power greater than any static your business can bug you with. You realize that help is on the way. It gives you strength to hang on, and maybe even to stand up straight and smile a little while you do— or at least to stop frowning and gritting your teeth quite so hard.

Here, if you wish, you can also enjoy the cleansing effect of sharing your shortcomings. Psychiatrists tell us we need sympathetic sounding boards, people willing to listen to problems and to whom we can actually confess our faults. James says, "Confess your faults one to another, and pray for one another, that ye may be healed. The effectual fervent prayer of a righteous man availeth much" (5:16). Sometimes you may feel that you are "righteous" as you pray for someone else who has shared a problem. At other times you will not feel righteous at all, but you will find practical, specific aids to everyday living, which have worked in the lives of others. You will find that these "peculiar" people, of whom you are one, is a group with plenty of humor, because, like anyone dealing with the big issues of life, they turn to humor to see them through strenuous times.

Harold Wildish, a witty English missionary to Jamaica, tells young people how to refuse a drink: "Just politely say, 'No, thank you.' If they ask the second time, just say 'No,' and if they persist the third time shout 'NO!' "

We call N. B. Hord, a retired carpenter who is a member of our church, our Will Rogers or Mark Twain. He quotes the Bible, but also from his own collection of quotations he likes to quote statements such as:

"Feed your faith, and your fear will starve to death."

"You can swallow your pride if you chew on it a
   while."

"You'll never get ahead by trying to get even."

Sometimes when you're seeking Christ's answer
to a problem, you are aided in finding it by looking
through the eyes of such brothers as this and others
who reflect Christ in their lives, helping us trans-
late heavenly guidance into action we can understand and use.

But there's a third wonder drug also dispensed
at prayer meetings, and that's the renewed realiza-
tion of how fortunate you are. You hear the problems of others and realize you aren't so bad off.
When you begin to think and pray about other
folks' problems, you begin to take on a mysterious
strength to handle your own. I can't explain it. I
just experience it. So will you when you start taking
advantage of prayer meeting, "Praying always with
all prayer and supplication in the Spirit, and watching thereunto with all perseverance and supplication for all saints" (Eph. 6:18).

"OK," you say. "I'll give it a go. I said I want to
go the route, and I will, if it kills me. I'll tiptoe into
prayer meeting among the little old ladies in tennis
shoes and see what happens. Does that complete
my course?"

Patience, friend. There's more, but thousands
have taken the next step without harmful effects,
and you can too. In fact, when you find what it's
all about, you'll really want to. Before I mention
it, though, let me say that you may find others at
prayer meeting besides little old ladies. At ours, for
example, you'll quite often see the head of a busy
air-conditioning and refrigeration business, a vice
president of a bank, and a man who owns three
restaurants. These are all successful he-man types.

At Home, Too?

Now for that other item I was going to mention. It's Bible reading and family devotions.

"Bible reading?" you gulp. "I don't mind once in a while looking up a passage like you've been quoting, but to read it from cover to cover—"

I didn't say cover to cover. You may want to eventually. But start with easy passages. Work into it gradually. If you have a family, you'll have help, because one good way to make sure you read the Bible every day is to get the whole family into the act. They need it too, you know. If you are a parent of small children, once you start the daily reading, they will remind you to do it.

There's another benefit in the whole family reading together: you get to see each other, know each other, learn what's going on in minds and hearts around the breakfast table where you read. Yes, that's the place. Do it first thing after breakfast. Then it gets done. Don't read much. Five to a dozen verses is usually enough. You can get a daily Bible reading guide or set of suggested readings from Sunday School literature or a religious book store. A quick, simple, and effective method is for Mother or Dad to read aloud while the others listen. After the reading, you and each member of the family in turn pray a short prayer aloud—anything the Lord puts into your heart.

How does all this help in business? It helps clear the family air of little problems that can nag folks during the day if they're not settled. Take them to God. He can work on them during the day while you concentrate on business. The morning devotion also gives you a surge of strength when you hear members of your family pray for you. It buoys you up with love and helps you rise above petty things. It strengthens you against temptation and discouragement. Your family believes in you. How can you not believe in yourself? It strengthens your resolve to come through for them. You're also strengthened when you pray for them. You are voicing your faith that God will handle things. "If God be for us . . ."

Finally, the morning family devotion helps keep things in perspective. You are reminded of your role in the family and in life. You realize that what may be vital to you is not of much concern to others, and what is nothing to you is real to them, and you had better rethink some attitudes or you will hurt someone. Warning flags may be unconsciously raised by prayers, indicating a family discussion may be due this evening. Perhaps a few words right after the morning devotion may make this day a glad one instead of a bad one.

If you live alone, you do not need to read aloud or pray aloud, but you do need to be as regular with the reading and prayer as the family person. You may also eventually want to form a Bible-reading and prayer partnership with a neighbor.

I have outlined the basic tools you need in developing your Christian approach to business: Regular weekly Sunday School, worship, and prayer meeting attendance, Bible reading, prayer, and family devotions.

Now, how do these tools work?

5

Be Determined

"And it came to pass, when the time was come that He should be received up, He steadfastly set his face to go to Jerusalem" (Luke 9:51). Jesus approached His divine work with determination.

With this chapter we start what you might call a series of "*Be* Attitudes." They're attitudes or policies you'll need if you want to succeed in business while holding firm to your Christian convictions. The first one, "Be Determined," is a requirement for success in anything. Keep on keeping on, never giving up, everlastingly trying, and trying again. You've heard all the slogans and mottoes, but what you need is everlasting *energy* to keep you supplied so you can keep going when everyone and everything around you shouts, "Give up! It ain't worth it!"

Well, good news! This energy supply is built into the tools listed in the last chapter: Prayer, Bible study, worship, faith, and fellowship. The daily devotions with Bible reading and prayer are the ignition keys that get the day started. The Bible is the giant storage battery that runs your motor.

Since prayer is so important, we must take time here to give you some details on its use. Psalm 55:17 says, "Evening, and morning, and at noon, will I pray, and cry aloud: and He shall hear my voice." In the busy advertising world, there is *pressure*. Deadlines, requests for help on projects for other departments or public service jobs, new assignments almost every day, and the whole thing beclouded with personnel problems and other tensions. I would bow my head at my desk the first thing in the morning and ask the Lord to help me, not only to do the work but to hold my temper and keep my sanity and sense of humor. And I would ask Him to help me advise others who came to me with their problems. "My voice shalt Thou hear in the morning, O Lord; in the morning will I direct my prayer unto Thee, and will look up" (Ps. 5:3).

Notice the emphasis on *morning*. What time do you start work? Ed Soistman, a 35-year veteran at Martin Marietta Corporation, starts at 8:18 A.M. That may seem an odd hour, but that's the way his company has its time units arranged. However, Ed is there by about 7 A.M., reading the Bible. He reads from three to five chapters every day and is now reading through his fifth version of the Bible. Ed feels he has some catching up to do. He was not saved until he was 40 years old. As assistant controller of Planning and Cost Control and Management Systems of this giant aerospace company, Ed has a big job—188 people working for him. If a man with this type of responsibility feels it's important to begin the day with the Bible, what about you?

I read my Bible at home. You set up a schedule that best fits you. The idea is to let God get His Word in before the world crowds in on you. Then, no matter what happens during the day you can remember His Word and see if you're still with Him. Then, notice, too, in that first reference, that you can do it again at noon and at night. You need spiritual food all day, as you do physical food.

Handling the Pressures

You probably don't have time to read the Bible once the day roars in upon you. All you'll have time to do is hold conferences, give orders, take orders, take calls, make calls, make decisions, make trips, make money, work, Work, WORK! That's what you're paid to do.

But through it all, you can pause every now and then and breathe a prayer, for yourself or someone else, and try to remember something of the Scriptures you read at the start of the day. Here, again, your basic tools come in. If you are regular in Sunday School, worship, prayer meeting, and family devotions, you'll find these little prayers come more easily, more naturally. You'll find it's possible to pray for someone instead of cursing him. Weird? Far out? Maybe, but you're one of the "peculiar" ones, remember? If we had more such peculiar people there would be fewer business and government scandals, and fewer heads rolling.

In the busy collections department of Orlando's Florida National Bank, each ring of Vice President Walter Barnes' phone means he must make a fast decision. Here is a man under pressure. He's a happy, stockily-built, Santa Claus type fellow, with a ready smile and laugh. On Sundays he teaches a Sunday School class and directs our church choir. He reads the Bible every morning before he goes to work, and he has a Bible at his desk.

Walter takes time on his way into the office each day to speak pleasantly to the janitor. With decision after decision zinging at Walter, he needs a built-in tranquilizer. He has found it in brief silent prayers. He may utter one as he burrows into his stack of mail each morning, saying, "Lord, You know which ones need to pay up today." Or he may briefly pray just before a conference, or during one, whether it's a meeting of several people or of only one or two at his desk. Walter says that these prayers work! "I have seen too many things work out so much better than I could have done it on my own, it *had* to be the work of the Lord," he declares. "If we are doing something for His glory, He will help us. He doesn't want His children to fail!"

Handling Failure

What? You tried everything I've mentioned, and it didn't work? You started off happy and confident Monday morning with prayer in your mind and some solid Bible verses under your belt, but by noon somebody had blasted your whole spirit from under you? You tried it again the next day and for a whole week or a whole month, and somebody or something always smashed you flat and left you looking like an idiot? You lost your temper, you swore, you made rotten remarks about someone, you goofed off, you lied about something?

Welcome, friend. I have failed too.

That's not the point. The point is how many times did you try *again* to do it God's way? How many days did you start off again with the family devotion, the Bible reading, the prayers, the whole thing, and the renewed determination to do it better *today*? *That's* the *payoff*. That's the answer to whether you're really beginning to get the formula. If you gave up after a week or month or 10 years, you need to keep reading this chapter. The title, remember: "Be Determined." If you're determined, you just keep on . . . forever.

Dr. John Johns, president of Stetson University, tells a story of the farmer who had lost only a few hogs during a severe cholera epidemic. The county agent asked the farmer if he had learned anything about the course of the disease, and he replied, "Wal, ah've noticed that them as gits it and lingers a spell has a better chance of livin' than them that dies right off." Don't die right off! Stick in there.

When I was sports editor of an army newspaper, covering boxing, I learned that the most aggressive fighters did not always win. The ability on the part of the defensive ones to "take it" often seemed to be a most valuable asset to winning. The aggressive man quite often wore himself out hammering on the tough fellow who just seemed to stand there like a great boulder and not throw many punches —at least for a long while. Then, after the vigorous upstart had worn himself into fatigue by constant flailing, the slow but durable boxer would suddenly uncork a wallop or two that would flatten his over-eager opponent. How's your staying power?

The army command for green troops who needed to start over on a marching exercise they had goofed was, "Fall back and regroup!" That's what you have to do time and time again, day in, day out, year in and year out. It's what Isaiah meant when he said, "They that wait upon the Lord shall renew their strength; they shall run, and not be weary; and they shall walk, and not faint" (Isa. 40:31).

When you blow your top or fail to witness, or

SUCCESSFUL LIVING
"Family Reading Centers"

Your Personal
Book Mark

Thank you for buying this book! Please help us serve you better by completing and mailing this card!

___ I buy Successful Living books at _____

_____

___ I've complimented the store manager for carrying these inspirational, family-type books!

___ I found the Book Rack in good order.

___ I enjoy reading this type of literature. Please send me your **catalog**.

___ I would appreciate spiritual counseling toward a more real and personal relationship with God.

___ I will support your ministry with prayer.

___ My church or group would like to have a Rack.

___ Please send details on how to become a Distributor.

___ Please send details on how I can have a Successful Living Party in my home.

NAME_____

ADDRESS_____

_____ ZIP _____

PHONE (___)_____

". . . if you confess with your mouth, 'JESUS IS LORD,' and believe in your heart that God raised HIM from the dead, you will be saved. For it is with your heart that you believe and are justified, and it is with your mouth that you confess and are saved. Everyone who calls on the name of the Lord will be saved." Romans 10:9-10, 13 [New International Version]

WHAT IS SUCCESSFUL LIVING?

We're an organization which takes a positive action distributing inspirational books through dedicated independent Distributors. Want to participate? We have a plan!

WHY THIS EMPHASIS?

"If religious books are not widely circulated among the masses in this country, I do not know what is going to become of us as a nation. If truth be not diffused, error will be; if God and His Word are not known and received, the devil and his works will gain the ascendancy; if the evangelical volume does not reach every hamlet, the pages of a corrupt and licentious literature will; if the power of the Gospel is not felt throughout the length and breadth of the land, anarchy and misrule, degradation and misery, corruption and darkness, will reign without mitigation or end."

— *Daniel Webster, 1823*

CALL OR WRITE TODAY!
Your Successful Living Distributor

JOAN & JACK GIVEN
1115 Institute St.
Valparaiso, Indiana 46383
Phone: (219) 462-7135
DISTRIBUTORS FOR S   L

when you actually deny the Lord, what do you do? Quit? Never! "Cast thy burden upon the Lord, and He shall sustain thee: He shall never suffer the righteous to be moved" (Ps. 55:22).

You have failed, but you have not failed *forever!* God knows that you failed, but He also knows that you tried to serve Him. You started in the right direction, even though you were diverted by yourself or someone else, maybe even something mechanical like a car that wouldn't start or a movie projector bulb that blew in the middle of a big presentation, or a power failure that shut down the plant when you were already behind on a big order.

Bouncing Back

When you fail God, ask His forgiveness. A good prayer for such a miserable spot is Psalm 25:18. "Look upon mine affliction and my pain; and forgive all my sins." Then we have His assurance: "If we confess our sins, He is faithful and just to forgive us our sins, and to cleanse us from all unrighteousness" (1 John 1:9).

Besides asking forgiveness of God, how about apologizing to someone you've wronged? It's not easy and not always possible, but when you can do it, it usually improves human relations. Apologies can set off all kinds of reactions. One is to produce a feeling of gratefulness and kindness in the person to whom you apologize. This feeling is so strong that it "makes the day" for that person, and may vastly improve all the contacts he or she has with other people.

Your apology may come as such a shock that it produces other results. The person may apologize to you, may even suddenly pour out a whole stream of apologies and confessions for other incidents.

Another effect of an apology may be a slow, careful reappraisal of your whole character by the other person. Apologies are so scarce these days that sometimes they set people to studying us with great curiosity. It takes strength and courage to apologize. They'll wonder where you got yours, and will be watching you closely to see if you ever apologize again.

Having asked forgiveness of God and of others, and having done what you could to repair the damage of your pagan-type failure, all you need to do is to have faith and determination to try again, believing that you will do better.

It doesn't sound like much to go on, but it's enough. God knows we are imperfect. He does not ask the impossible. At this point, too many people make the mistake of crucifying themselves when God wants them only to forgive themselves. Naturally you hate what you have done and hate yourself for doing it. But, having hated, having made corrections, *drop* it! Onward and upward! Corny as that may sound, it's the only way.

One reason so few people try to live by God's law and Christ's mercy is that they think anything that simple can't be adequate. Why do we always keep looking for something complicated? True, we use only 2% or 5% of our brain power (whichever expert you listen to) but God knew that we would operate this way, so He made His way simple. He wanted *children* to learn it, so He made it simple enough for them. Why spend your life searching for something you already have? You want a sure-fire, iron-clad, guaranteed, fail-safe, fool-proof formula for everything? You've *got* it. Now *do* it. *Live* it.

"But wait," you say. "I am *doing* it! I *didn't* give up. I've been living all my life by the simple way you outline. I'm *still* a failure in business. I'm a Christian, and everybody looks up to me, but I've never achieved success. I've got the same little old piddling job I've had all these years and what has it gotten me? What good am I to myself or family or anyone else?"

There are two answers to that. Either you are more successful than you realize, or you can have more success—if not here, then elsewhere.

Success in Disguise

First, are you actually better off than you think? What do you count success? Money? Prestige? Security? Happiness? *Whose* happiness? Yours or your family's? Why did you take that job in the first place? What was attractive about it? Why have you stayed? What advantages do you have that someone in another job or another business does not have? I have often been tempted to envy someone else, but when I stopped to analyze whether I would really trade jobs, I have decided, "Thanks, but no, thanks." The other job paid more, but on it I would have to travel more, deal with people whose policies or personalities I didn't enjoy, and do other things I disliked.

Quite often we become dissatisfied if someone new is brought in over us. We say, "Why, *I* should have had that job." But if we will look closely at the job, we'll decide that even though it might have been a promotion, it would have brought duties and responsibilities we really don't want. The reason a person is not promoted may be that he has not actually *worked* for promotion. He has been faithful in his job, but he has never tried to work up to the *next* job. And he has perhaps subconsciously even resisted the idea of moving up because he knows he could not be happy in a bigger job.

If this is your situation and you feel you have failed by not climbing as high as you could, think again. You have at least succeeded where you are. If you had failed, you would have been gone. Now is your present spot so bad, after all? You have a steady income and are doing your bit for the company. You are providing for your family and paying your bills. You may have a greater measure of security than many "big shots." Often, if things go badly for a company, it is the top people who are the first to fall. And it is sometimes harder for them to find positions once they are out.

But suppose you really did deserve the promotion? You know and everyone else—maybe even your boss—admits that you should have had the new spot, and you really worked for it. You were qualified and were ready to move up to the bigger responsibility, longer hours, and everything that came with it. Then the boss says, "I hate to tell you this. But the parent company is sending down someone to take over the spot I wanted you to have."

You have two alternatives. One is to stay and "take it." If you feel God wants you to stay, be sure that you do. If you have resentment, commit the situation to Him and He will remove your resentment. But you must truly be willing to give it up and not nurse it. Get your eyes off your own hurt feelings and onto what you can do to make the new man's acceptance easier. Company loyalty and cooperation are ideal ways to show Christian love.

Success Without Promotions

What about the other alternative—trying something, or somewhere, else? A man I knew who worked on a newspaper was discouraged because an outsider had been brought in over him. The long-time employee knew in his heart that he would not have wanted that job. Still, the principle of the thing rankled him. He would have liked the boss at least to offer him the job as a show of confidence in his capability. He stewed over the situation until he decided he could not live with it, though he knew he still had a good deal even without the promotion. He could not be loyal to the new man because he could not respect the new man's character. So he gave up 15 years' seniority, and went into business for himself.

This man did not fail on his long-time job. Nor did he fail when he changed jobs. But he well might have failed if he had been given the job above him—not because he couldn't handle it, but because his heart would not have been in it!

Right here is where a lot of people get off the track to true success. The boss *does* give them the chance to move up, and they make the move, never stopping to think whether the promotion is something they really want. They take it just because it's a promotion. Then they find they are no longer doing what they enjoy and what brought them the success they had.

Instead of being a happy office worker, for example, a person becomes an unhappy office manager, burdened with all the problems of personnel, supply, communications, and liaison with top management. A production worker becomes foreman, with all the headaches of work planning, a department quota to meet, and trying to find fill-in people when someone calls in sick. A salesman becomes sales manager and faces the responsibility of training and disciplining a whole sales force. Instead of the free and easy outside life of selling—which he loved—he finds himself imprisoned behind a desk, bogged down in paper shuffling and people shuffling—which he hates.

Success is not necessarily climbing the ladder as high as you can go just to be climbing. Success is achieving a happy adjustment to life where you can serve God, others, and your own best interests.

Success Involving a Change

But suppose you want a job that's better than the one you have—or at least different. Suppose that where you are you cannot have the success you want on the terms you know God wants you to have it. What then? You can either try to change yourself, change the people and the situation where you are, or move. Can you work harder, be more outgoing, ask for more responsibility, take additional training, or do something else to make yourself more valuable? Or is there absolutely no place to go but out? Whichever course you decide God wants you to follow, you must use determination. "Brethren, I count not myself to have apprehended; but this one thing I do, forgetting those things which are behind, and reaching forth unto those things which are before, I press toward the mark for the prize of the high calling of God in Christ Jesus" (Phil. 3:13-14).

No matter how many times you are defeated or rebuffed, you have only to bounce back one more time than you're knocked down. My father left a fairly secure job in an electrical workshop at age 56 because he was not happy. He started over again in spite of the fact that he was crippled and might have difficulty climbing ladders and doing other heavy physical work required on commercial electrical construction. He succeeded in making more money than he had ever made before in his life, and he was really happy in his work for the first time in 20 years!

If you are successful where you are and do not feel the need to move but would like a little more happiness and interest injected into the daily grind, here's just the thing for you: "Finally, brethren, whatsoever things are true, whatsoever things are honest, whatsoever things are just, whatsoever things are pure, whatsoever things are lovely, whatsoever things are of good report; if there be any virtue, and if there be any praise, think on these things" (Phil. 4:8).

That's what is known as positive thinking. Looking on the bright side of things on your job. Looking at the doughnut instead of the hole, the silver lining instead of the dark cloud. That's not very popular with some people (the losers!). It's considered naïve, square, or dull. That's one reason we have so many mixed-up people and such a mixed-up world. If you want a fresh start, but don't want to leave where you are, take a fesh start each morning—and as often as you can throughout the day. You can determine your own success—the way you want it, if it's the way God wants it and if you'll be determined!

"For the Lord God will help me; therefore shall I not be confounded: therefore have I set my face like a flint, and I know that I shall not be ashamed" (Isa. 50:7).

Now *that's* determination! Hard as flint! Our determination has to be hard as flint; but our approach to people in carrying it out needs to be gentle, as we are about to see.

6

Be Gentle

People don't listen with their ears; they listen with their hearts.

I once had to caution a young executive who had recently taken over a department. He was using his new authority with a heavy hand. He was making enemies by ordering people around with harsh commands when the situation did not require it. "Throwing your weight around" can result from nervousness about new responsibility, an eagerness to show leadership, or the sheer joy of a new position of command. Guard against it.

Another situation requiring gentleness arises when you are tempted to overreact to a small injustice, or an apparent one. One company I worked for had a handy parking space under a shelter next to the building. I had parked there for some time when a new "young tiger" executive joined the company in another department, and was assigned the place. I was asked if it didn't irk me. I pointed out to my questioner two facts: (1) The company did not recognize seniority in matters of this kind, but only rank. Since this new man outranked me, the privileged parking space was definitely his; I was not being done an injustice. (2) The issue of a parking space was so trivial it should upset no one, even if an injustice had occurred.

Gentle Subordination

Akin to this situation was one in which an outsider was brought in over several men, each of whom thought he should have been promoted to head the department. Though all were disappointed, one pointed out to the others that there was no use bucking the new man. It was not his fault that he had been assigned to this unhappy situation. He, like those beneath him, had a job to do. In a sense he was under as much pressure as any of them— perhaps more. Why make it worse by fighting him?

Incidentally, this problem of having someone brought in over you is more common than you might realize. If it happens to you, do not consider it a disgrace or an unforgivable mistreatment. It happens all the time. It once happened to me. In talking with men in various fields, I found it can happen just about anywhere.

It is, in fact, sometimes a necessity. You never know when someone is going to come along who is so much better qualified for a job than you are that the boss is compelled to give him preference. The boss' job is to keep the business operating at top efficiency. He cannot let you be promoted if there is someone else who can do the job better, or if someone is specified for the job by your boss' boss, regardless of qualifications!

A Southern-born educational administrator with a master's degree and more than 40 years experience served faithfully during the troublous period of the 1960s, carrying out a desegregation program in deep south communities. Now he finds the man over him is a black educator with less professional and administrative experience than he has. What is his reaction? "I just go ahead and do my own work as a Christian and as a professional educator with the sole objective of serving the boys and girls."

Gentle Administration

This educator's gentle Christian attitude passed the test in another crisis situation—a teachers' walkout. Though, as administrator, he was on the side of "management," he was so respected by those participating in the walkout that he received appreciative letters from its leaders for the attitude of the administration during the crisis.

One of the most common causes of friction—and therefore of fireworks—is losing your gentleness after a long buildup of frustrations and releasing your anger at a completely innocent person. You can guard against this by stopping when you think you are about to reach the breaking point. Say to yourself, "Wait a minute! This next person doesn't have anything at all to do with what's happened to me before!"

Stop thinking about all the gunners who have shot you down today. Lean back and relax for a minute. Take a few deep breaths. Think about God, the Bible, the church, your family, and maybe something like a cool mountain stream, the seashore, a nice day on the golf course, or something else pleasant and calming. Then think about this innocent person you're going to talk to next.

If you head a business or a department, can you be gentle and still keep your people working? "Yes," says Ed Soistman. "Level with people. Communicate. Tell them as much as you can. Build up trust. This way they are on your side. They really want to help you. They'll work harder for you because they respect you."

Walt Barnes adds, "When you do your best, they in turn want to do their best. Be consistent."

Gentle Termination

But suppose their best is not good enough. Can you *fire* someone gently? The president of a busy Chicago typesetting and graphics business has found you can. His industry is unionized, as he puts it, "to the eyeteeth." The union protects employees so carefully that a discharged one may sometimes have to be reinstated with all back pay.

This executive points out that, conditions being what they are, it is all the more important for him to be gentle. He has found that, by exercising great patience and trying to see a situation as God does, he can be gentle at the same time he is "laying it on the line" to an unsatisfactory employee. On one such occasion, a man who was dismissed admitted that he had not been producing. After he was gone he bore no grudge, even sending the executive a Christmas card with the message, "You're the greatest."

Firing someone, of course, is not necessarily all bad. If done in a positive, constructive, sympathetic manner, you can make the employee see that he or she is perhaps not cut out for this type of work and can be more effective and successful elsewhere. Many executives, through contacts in other fields, are successful in getting employees new job opportunities before they even fire them.

As an employer or manager you can do more than you realize to establish a tone of gentility about your whole business, even in a business which may generally be considered tough. Take the case of Allen Trovillion, for example, who has a thriving contracting firm. While in college contemplating the building business, he almost changed his major because the picture he got of the people in the trade was that they were a hard-drinking, rough-talking, and tough-acting bunch. Once he decided he could succeed without all that, however, he went ahead, and for 20 years he has succeeded very well.

Gentle Consternation

This amazing Christian contractor must have learned patience from Job himself. Or perhaps it was a Trovillion ancestor from whom Job learned patience! What would you do if one of your construction hands put 50 yards of concrete up in forms —wrong? The mistake cost $10,000, but Allen Trovillion didn't rant, rave, chew the man out, and fire him. "He saw his mistake," Trovillion explained. "Naturally I was disappointed, but there was no need to explode."

So, whatever your business—or your position in it—be as easy to get along with as you can. "Rejoice with them that do rejoice, and weep with them that weep" (Rom. 12:15). So you didn't get a raise but someone else did. Congratulate the lucky party if it's mentioned. And if someone else gets a tough break of some kind, don't be afraid to show some sympathy. We never know the burdens people bear, and we never know how much a kind word of understanding will help. The world is full of people who want only to be noticed, to have the feeling that somebody—anybody—cares they exist.

To Ed Soistman come not only people in his own department, but others who have been referred to him. The need for personal Christian counseling seems so great he has sometimes considered leaving his present work and giving full time to helping people with their problems.

Walter Barnes says that a former bank officer sometimes calls him for some Christian advice. For a long time in one place I worked, I thought I was the only person being sought out for Christian discussions. Then I learned that there were at least two others, and they were also surprised that there were so many people seeking fundamental Christian advice to solve problems of daily living.

Some of the questions you get are far removed from anything serious, but there is within them a startling warning of how little some people know of God's Word. Gazing at a fish mounted on an office wall, a fellow once asked me, "Do you think that fish had a soul?" That was spoken pretty much in jest, but another executive once asked me in all seriousness if Santa Claus is in the Bible. Another man who said he had once been active in church spied a paperback copy of the Psalms in my office once and said, "Ah, yes, the *Palms!*"

After a few experiences like that, you begin to feel like an expert, from sheer contrast with the unbelievable Bible ignorance all around. Naturally, there are also many sharp-shooter types who try to make you feel like an idiot by popping the famous question of "Where did Cain's wife come from?" and other awkward impertinencies. These people may be only kidding or may be testing you to see how your Christian gentility holds up under pressure.

Gentle Consultation

Among the people who come to you, however, you

will also find a great many who are genuinely troubled about something and who are eager to get help they feel you can provide. You may find yourself becoming something of a counselor, an unofficial chaplain. (Many companies today, realizing that the need for counseling is great, are actually hiring chaplains.) Naturally you have to be very careful in giving out free advice; some of it may be acted upon! So stick closely to the basic rules of Christian conduct. Stay with general principles such as advising prayer for people who have wronged those who consult you, or prayer for the office situation, or patience and "going the second mile" in various conflict situations. Naturally, you will also observe the basic common sense rules of human relations:

Never make a judgment without hearing both sides of the story.

Never speak derogatorily of anyone.

Keep the discussion as positive and optimistic as possible.

Unless you are a trained minister, physician, psychologist, or sociologist, you will realize right off that you are in water over your head. Your role of unofficial counselor has been thrust upon you simply because you have shown by your life that you have more spiritual qualities than others in the place seem to have. So, take a lesson from the experienced counselors who tell us, "Most people who come for counseling want only one thing— somebody to talk to, somebody who will listen. Merely voicing their problems helps them begin to straighten things out. This is the first time some of these people have had a chance to examine their problems by talking them out. Sometimes about all you have to do is listen."

A psychiatrist, addressing a group of executives, gave them a little basic training in helping other people. He said, "If somebody comes to you with a problem, all you do at first is listen. Sometimes I listen for 20 minutes. Then, when the person pauses for breath, I say, 'Hmmmmm.' Then I listen for another 20 minutes, and when he pauses again, I say, 'Hmm, you surely do have a problem.' Then after he finally talks himself out, I say, 'Well, what do you think you should do?' He tells me, and the chances are it is a very good solution, just about exactly what I would recommend, at least from the facts he has given me. 'Well,' I say, 'that sounds feasible. Why don't you try that and see how it works? If it doesn't work out, come back and we'll talk again.' By this time he is relieved, happy and even enthusiastic to go and try the solution *he has worked out, merely by talking about the problem and seeing it in its entirety for the first time*. Then he shakes hands and thanks me for being so helpful!"

In my counseling sessions I remembered this advice, and it always worked out this way. If these people potentially had the answers to their own problems all the time, why did they come to me? I was gentle with my Christian approach to life and to them. I had shown that I had a certain serenity, a "grip on things" that seems to be rare in the rush and tumble of the business world. Many have such inner resources but are afraid to show it outside of church or their homes. In business they think you have to be tough, on your guard, unapproachable.

I used some company time listening to people. But they had problems, and they found answers by talking them out. It helped keep them on an even keel; helped clear tension from the air; and helped people clear their minds so they could work more effectively. People are what make business, and if we can keep them running smoothly, the business will run well too.

So, be gentle. The big rule to keep in mind, of course, is the Golden Rule. If *you* were that problem person, how would *you* want to be approached and treated? What would make you shape up and help your situation? Keep that in mind and do all that you do in *love*. Too much "religion" or "preaching"—too soon or of the wrong kind—on the job can be sand in the gears. Don't be sand. Be oil. There is a way to do this. It may not come naturally to you, but it can be learned. Sometimes you have to be lubricating oil, sometimes penetrating oil. How does one do it? By being subtle.

7

Be Subtle

Jesus tells us how to be subtle: "Behold I send you forth as sheep in the midst of wolves: be ye therefore wise as serpents, and harmless as doves" (Matt. 10:16).

Wise and harmless, He says. How do you get wise? Well, you're probably already wise enough. Most of us just don't use the wisdom we have. We don't take time to think! So that's the first step in being subtle: Thinking . . . planning . . . determining how to act logically, intelligently, and efficiently.

But what about the second quality specified—harmless? You must consider feelings as well as facts. You must weigh possible benefits of your plans against potential harm. Is there any likelihood that what you plan may be misunderstood? Are you setting a precedent for future action that may cause a problem if you have to repeat it—or find you *cannot* repeat it? Consider all angles.

One of the most delicate jobs in business is that of the secretary. The busy executive can't talk to just anybody and everybody, every time. He must be protected. So the secretary is caught in the middle. She must find out who is calling, find out whether the boss wants to talk to that person, and at the same time keep everybody happy. Thus, the magnificent line, "May I *tell* him who's calling?" She doesn't say that she'll ask if he wants to talk, or that she'll see if he's in. All the poor girl asks is that you identify yourself—a fair enough request. Wise as a serpent, harmless as a dove.

Subtle Is Not Stupid

A Christian industrialist who prefers to remain anonymous said, "We must study people and try to meet them where they are. Some have no concept of spiritual things. We must try to develop some kind of common understanding before we can reach them."

Walter Barnes, the banker, adds that we must get to know the person *firsthand* and not merely gather information from others.

Yet, taking a real interest in some people is not easy. Some have been so hurt that they resist any attempt to penetrate their lives. You may have to work very slowly. A drop of kindness and concern here, a smile there, a greeting, an occasional word of encouragement, a gift, an occasional lunch together—any or all of these may eventually begin to soften the toughest person.

Barnes has found that one subtle way of helping a person is by explaining how he solved a problem similar to the one that person faces. Another thing he does is to find reliable professional counselors who are Christians. There is a pastor, for example, to whom he can refer someone who comes to him with a problem about alcoholism.

If more people took the time to think and pray about problems, there wouldn't be so many problems. God gave us the ability to think so that we can solve or prevent problems.

Often, though, as Manley Beasley says, "Your problem isn't your problem. Your problem is you!" A good honest session of prayer and confession, claiming 1 John 1:9, might do more for the situation than anything else.

All right, let's say you are right with the Lord and there's *still* a problem. "If any of you lack wisdom, let him ask of God, that giveth to all men liberally, and upbraideth not, and it shall be given him" (James 1:5). Colossians 4:5-6 also has some light for you: "Walk in wisdom toward them that are without, redeeming the time. Let your speech be always with grace, seasoned with salt, that ye may know how ye ought to answer every man."

A man who had taken over a business from someone else found himself in a rather ticklish spot at times because he did not know exactly what to charge for various services. He did have the grace that Colossians speaks of, however, and found that it helped him feel his way to the answers he needed. When a client would come in who had been a client of the previous owner and would ask what the charge would be, the new man would say, "Well, let's see, what was it last year? I can look it up, but if you remember, it will save us some time."

This did two things: (1) The client usually remembered, so this gave the man the information he needed. If the fee seemed enough, he could charge the same. If not, he had it as a base from which to charge an increase which would be acceptable, due to a current climate of rising costs in all fields. (2) His trusting in the client to quote the

correct figure helped to build goodwill and confidence.

Subtle Is Not Soft

You can be subtle and still, in a Christian way,
take a stand to insure your self-respect. Once I was
invited to a company social event which not only
had no appeal to me, but which would have been
an imposition and nuisance to my family. There was
no business reason for the event. It was a quickly-
hatched-up, spur-of-the-moment idea and not well
planned. I expressed my reply to the invitation in
this manner, "If my job depends on it, I'll go." This
subtle statement pretty well made clear how ridiculous such a requirement would be, and it got
me off the hook very neatly.

Years ago I heard a humorous illustration of how
an insurance man sells life insurance to a person
who is desperately afraid of death. His subtle line
was, "If you buy this policy today, then, if—God
forbid—in 120 years something should happen,
everything is taken care of." When dealing with
less touchy persons with whom the subject of death
could be more frankly discussed, he would naturally be a little more realistic. But his ability to shift
gears for the very frightened man showed the salesman's application of the principle Paul followed.
"To the weak became I as weak, that I might gain
the weak: I am made all things to all men, that I
might by all means save some" (1 Cor. 9:22).
Paul spoke of it in regard to saving souls, but it will
work for you in saving your job or in other business
problems.

In being all things to all men according to their
personalities, characters, and circumstances, you'll
find, for example, that with some blustery, egotistic

types you need to be as sincerely humble as you can. Other blustery ones like to be met with forcefulness. By a quiet firmness you can show you mean business and no monkey business.

A woman sales manager once issued a challenge to a group of sales people who needed some incentive. Though the approach did not seem subtle ("I'm sorry to say we'll have no Christmas party this year. Top management says we haven't earned it."), the method actually was very subtle. The immediate result of the blunt announcement was anger, but it soon turned to determination to sell more, just as the sales manager knew it would. Being familiar with the people involved, she knew this was the kindest approach because it would get her people working, and they would later thank her.

Sometimes it takes the simple spelling out of a situation to present a problem's solution most subtly. A man who sold his meat market assumed the unwarranted privilege of dropping by, taking what he wanted from the cooler, and telling the cashier what to charge him, without bothering to consult the new owner. When the new man told him there would be no more of that, the former owner invited him to remove his glasses and say that. "I'm not afraid of you," said the new owner, "but wouldn't it be stupid of us to grab these instruments here (indicating a meat cleaver and butcher knife) and make hash of each other?" The man decided it would indeed be stupid. He cooled off to the point of reasoning and agreed that from then on he would be served and receive a proper sales slip like any other customer.

Subtle Is Not Insensitive

To the weak, mild, and gentle you may have to

gear your approach down to your quietest self. Ironically, you may *not* have to, either. Sometimes earth's frightened, fragile people want someone who gives them security through a show of confident strength, a dynamic, "take-charge" person. But don't try to be that kind if you're one of earth's frightened, fragile ones yourself!

If you are a reserved, gentle type and don't want to flaunt power, you may need to be especially careful when in a position of leadership. One of the most adroit men I ever knew at making an employee feel at ease was a boss I had who gave me several raises. This may sound like the easiest thing a boss does, but it can be goofed like any other job if you handle it clumsily. This man, however, approached me in this way: "Well, how are things going? Are you happy here? How does your wife feel about the company? Well, we're glad you feel that way because we're happy with you, too. We're pleased to tell you that starting now your salary will be _____."

A man in another company commended me in equally as subtle a way for an extra job I had done on my own time. At least I had thought I was doing it on my own time. He was so pleased, however, that he not only paid me for the time but added a payment for lunch and tip! Both these men's approach had the subtle quality of making an employee feel that the boss had understanding, compassion, and a real interest in the employee's personal happiness and well-being; that he considered more than mere work accomplished; and was mindful also of the need for him to have a helpful attitude.

Some bosses are afraid to show anything other than an all-business manner. "You're getting a raise." That's it. The human computer has spoken. Never mind whether you've earned it; or earned more but this is all we can pay; or we're giving it to you because it's policy.

The supervisor in a boiler shop where I worked did not even tell me I was getting a raise. When I picked up my pay envelope, I asked if it was a raise or a mistake. "Whatsa matter," the man flung back, "don'tcha want it?"

I did, but it would also have been nice to have a kind word with it. Surely it would not have endangered the boss' job.

Subtle Is Not Striving

If you're dealing with a person who is all energy, you may either need to match that energy, or readily admit that you can *never* match it, thus complimenting the person by showing how valuable his trait is, if only he can control it. You can be subtle in praise if you are sincere. Praise is a form of recognition that is valuable in establishing and maintaining good relationships.

It is also possible to be subtle in offering a mild rebuke when necessary. After someone delivers a tirade against a person who perhaps does not deserve it, or in a situation where it is uncalled for and cannot possibly do any good, you can remark slyly, *"That'll* fix 'im!"

This shows the loudmouth that he is actually accomplishing nothing. Sometimes, when I have used this, the person has actually apologized. Usually there is at least a sheepish grin or a muttered, "Well, I guess I shouldn't have said that, but I just had to get it off my chest." These reactions are all implicit admissions that the tirade was to no real purpose.

The lazy person is another challenge to your understanding and love. You can use subtlety to motivate him to do his best. First, you must study him to see what will do the job. Fear of losing out? Shame (like a reminder of how he is cheating others by not doing his share)? Or sentiment (getting him to think how he is not being fair to his family when he goofs off)?

If a car is used in business it should be kept in top condition and appearance. When a lazy person comments, "Your car looks good. What do you do to it?" I reply, "Wash it." On modern finishes, that is about all you have to do so far as appearance is concerned if there are no damages to it. But this simple, subtle reply is enough to make the other person ask himself, "Hmmm. Point! When did I wash mine last?"

The discouraged or bored person sometimes needs only to be reminded of the larger vision of his mission. He is serving not only himself, but others in the company, in his family, community, and nation. He is part of something much bigger than himself. He sees only here and now; what of tomorrow and other opportunities that may be on the way? The smallest kind of subtle remark here can do wonders.

All some people need is to be reminded that they were looking for a job when they found this one, and that, bad though it is, it's better than what they had before, which was nothing. This does not work if thrown like a slap in the face. The subtle way is to quietly observe it as a one-two alternative that applies not only to the person involved but to yourself: "Well, we all have the same choice. We can stay or leave. That's the beauty of this country. Freedom."

Psychology is an unending study in itself, but if you take the time and trouble to seek how best to approach people with a view to helping them and the business situation, God will guide you to some basic points that will provide answers. Then you will do as well as could be expected under the circumstances, and probably a whole lot better.

8

Be Obvious

To me one of the most thrilling Gospel songs of recent years is "I'll Tell the World that I'm a Christian!" It boldly states the premise of the Christian speaking up for his faith, giving frank, open witness.

This part of the business-success-without-paganism formula is hard for many people. They are afraid to show their colors, take a stand, come right out and admit they are Christians.

If the idea makes you shudder, take a deep breath and read on anyhow. Nobody will see you, and maybe after you read this chapter, you'll see there's hope after all, even for timid you. The fact is, you've got muscle you may not realize. You don't really know your own strength. You can fly, brother!

"As for me and my house," said Joshua, "we will serve the Lord" (Josh. 24:15). Paul strengthened the Ephesians by this admonition, "Wherefore take unto you the whole armor of God, that ye may be able to withstand in the evil day, and having done all, to stand" (Eph. 6:13).

Evil day, did he say? Well, if it was any more evil then than now, I'm kind of glad we weren't there. We sure need God's armor today. What is it, anyhow? Let's look down a few more verses to Ephesians 6:17, "And take the helmet of salvation, and the sword of the Spirit, which is the Word of God." That's it! The Word! There are other pieces of armor for defense, but the Word is the only weapon listed for attack purposes. Just having a Bible on your desk or work bench, or having a New Testament or Gospel of John visible in your shirt pocket, will show whose side you're on.

Show Your Bible
I asked a variety of Christian businessmen how they make themselves known as Christians where they work. One of the most frequent answers was "Bible on the desk." It's a good start if you're new at trying to "tell the world that you're a Christian," and don't especially feel like speaking up about it for fear of being thought a hypocrite or religious fanatic. The Bible is a silent but very obvious testimony.

From bank to aerospace plant, I found the Bible on the desks of men who are courageous witnesses for Christ. At first it may take courage for you to put it there, if not right on the desk, perhaps on a side table or credenza close by, where it will be seen immediately. People will respect your courage for putting it there. It shows you have a strength they would like to have.

Moreover, the sight of the Bible is a sign that you can help them with answers to problems. People who have troubles and have tried a lot of unsuccessful ways to solve them often realize they need to go to God, but they don't know how to go about it. Seeing your Bible they say to themselves, "Hmmm, maybe this guy can explain to me where I can find the answers I need. It can't hurt to ask." And do they ask!

Soistman, the aerospace man, says, "Who does somebody go to with a problem? Not his neighbor. Not the family. If he is not a church-going person, he has no pastor to turn to. Going to a psychiatrist is frightening and expensive. So if he has in you a Christian business associate whom he respects, who has courage to refuse a drink, who doesn't run after his secretary, the chances are he'll come to you with his problem." At one time Ed was helping seven people with problems varying from juvenile delinquency to suicide threats. Some of the men who consult him are under such strain that their relief at being able to discuss their problems brings a burst of release in the form of tears.

Barnes, the banker, has likewise found that the presence of the Bible often prompts people to come to him with personal problems.

If you are the head of your own business, you may want to start the practice Don Mott has of not only having the Bible available, but reading it with your employees in the morning to start the day. He owns an insurance agency. One morning during the reading, two men came in and Don gave them a Bible so they could follow along with the reading. When it was over, one of the men said he didn't come in to talk insurance, but that from that moment on, the Mott agency would have his insurance business. He said, "I believe I have found an honest insurance agent. I don't believe a man would read the Bible with his staff and deal dishonestly with his policy holders." The contract? For 62 apartments!

So the Bible can bring you business, too. But that's not why you have it there. The reason is to help tell people you're a Christian and that here is help for them.

The head of a business can be bolder about creating a Christian atmosphere than someone who just works there. Yet he won't want to be heavy-handed about it. Don Mott doesn't insist that every person he hires be a Christian, but he does explain in advance the office custom of having daily Bible reading and prayer. If they can't accept that, they just don't want to join the company.

Use Christian Literature

Another much-used aid for witnessing on the job is the tract or printed testimony. Mott has written five of these. In a short space they give powerful witness that can be applied to many lives. Jim Burnett, who has an air-conditioning and refrigeration business, has had his personal testimony printed and gives it out by the hundreds. It's the exciting story of a Gulf of Mexico boating accident and what the terrifying experience did for him.

You may not have had any great, gripping Christianity-in-business experience to have printed in a tract to give out. You can, however, have a variety of inexpensive general tracts available to help testify to the principles you want to affirm. Tracts are available from churches and Christian bookstores as is other helpful literature. The very fact that you give out such literature is evidence of your stand.

The use of the Bible or other printed material to show that you are a Christian also does something for *you!* It strengthens you when people begin to identify you with Christ. They will respond to your stand, and it will show you *their need*. Ed Soistman relates how a man entered his office one morning during the pre-working hours when Ed reads the Bible. The man apologized for interrupting. "Not at all," Ed said. "I'm just reading about Daniel. Quite a story!"

"You know," said the man, "I've always wanted to start reading the Bible."

"Start now," said Ed, and he gave him a copy of a daily schedule for reading the Bible through in a year. No one had ever before given him this handy stimulus to get started.

A dynamic promoter of Christianity in his own business is Walt Meloon, now president of Correct Craft, a company which his father, W. C. Meloon, started. Meloon has evangelistic meetings in the plant and regularly shows Moody Science, Billy Graham, or Ken Anderson films. This has been a company practice for nearly 30 years. Employees are frequently presented Bibles or New Testaments. Recently they received *The Living Bible* and Hal Lindsey's books, *The Late Great Planet Earth*, and *Satan Is Alive and Well on Planet Earth*. Many employees have become such devoted Christians that they have left for the ministry or mission fields.

Meloon witnesses to customers and sends them a quarterly newspaper, each issue of which contains an article by Billy Graham. At the New York and Chicago boat shows, Meloon sponsors a breakfast for 100 or so boat buyers. There's a plug for Correct Craft, but the breakfast is given over largely to Christian testimony and music. Then there's a talk by some prominent Christian leader. Among those in the past have been George Beverly Shea, Cliff Barrows, Grady Wilson, and Jack Wyrtzen.

Laymen on the programs have included Richard Woike, vice president of National Liberty Life Insurance Company, Valley Forge, Pa.; and Waldo Yager, president of Courtland Produce Company, Toledo, Ohio, a former chairman of Christian Business Men's Committee, International.

Correct Craft doesn't operate on Sundays, even when an emergency order is being rushed through. "Experts" can't understand how it's done, but the company always gets the boats out on time. For a wartime contract they once put out 300 boats in a month. Normal capacity of the plant was 48.

One of the greatest tests of Meloon's Christianity in business was a six-year period of operating the company under Chapter 11 of the bankruptcy act. The situation was brought on by an unscrupulous government inspector who rejected boats which really had no flaws. The company proved what was happening by removing inspection marks on some of the boats which had been rejected, sending them back through inspection again, and seeing them passed. The rejection rate kept running so high, however, that the company's money became tied up in production and it could not pay its bills.

The story of the many miracles which saved the company is too long to recount here. Among them, however, was an emergency loan of $40,000 from Norway, a $139,000 order from Pakistan, and the eventual government repayment of $280,000 and complete admission of blame by the United States authorities.

How did Walt Meloon take all of this? "It gave me a ministry in bankruptcy," he pointed out. "As a result of what I went through, I have been able to be of great help and comfort to many businessmen who are going through bankruptcy." He has actually told the story all over the world!

Take Your Stand

Allen Trovillion gives his witness each year at his company's Christmas party, letting the people there know exactly where he stands. He was one of only three men in his entire college fraternity who didn't drink. When he started his contracting business, he determined to keep his high standards. In a business that is notorious for its rough talking, job-hopping men, strikes, and violence, Trovillion has a high percentage of Christians and plenty of employee loyalty. Some of his people have been with him since the company started in 1953. He makes it clear to everyone that he doesn't care for profanity, and that it isn't necessary. Everyone at Trovillion's has pride in the company. There's never been a strike.

An incident from Trovillion's life, incidentally, illustrates the point that making yourself obvious and visible as a Christian may be as simple as taking a firm ethical stand on business questions. When a man asked him for a sizable sum of money in order to swing a big, juicy series of contracts his way, Trovillion made it clear that he had no need of buying business. The would-be briber's company, by the way, later went broke. Trovillion once turned down a $2 million job because a client wanted him to short-cut quality on it. He turned down a $3 million job because he was convinced that the business the man wanted the building for could never succeed. The customer later made sounder arrangements and awarded Trovillion another contract.

The Chicago graphics firm president, mentioned earlier, is another executive who has squarely faced the under-the-table-payments problem and found he has suffered no ill effects from turning down such deals. He also made his ethical stand obvious in a courageous manner when he turned down an order from a longtime customer. The material was pornographic, and though he risked losing the customer, he refused the job. The customer said he understood, and the fact that the job was turned down raised his respect for the company. He is still a good customer.

People Will Come to You

Once you begin to make yourself known as a Christian, things will start happening to make you *better* known. One of the most common of these is a request for you to give the invocation at some occasion. Once you do that, you have given public evidence of being a praying person. Do not be surprised if some day shortly after that someone comes to you for some spiritual or personal advice. His approach to you may be shy and awkward, and your response may be just as difficult. But if you offer a quick, silent prayer, you will find something to say. It may not seem adequate, but to the person in distress it may be a great turning point— merely because you have taken the time to listen, and, by that, shown that you want to help.

Ed Soistman tells of a brilliant scientist with a Ph.D. degree who came to him in a highly agitated state. The man's teenage daughter was threatening to run away. Ed offered the best advice he could as to a strategy for dealing with the girl. Two days later the man returned happy and relieved. All was well.

In another case a man whose father was dying of cancer in a distant city consulted Ed. He had determined that when his father died he would go to the funeral alone. This upset his wife and family. The wife called Ed about it. About all Ed could recommend was that she and the family pray about it and he promised to do likewise. It worked out. Eventually the man changed his mind and took the family along.

In an unusual case, Ed was asked to give the graveside eulogy for a former Marine he had won to the Lord. It was a full military funeral, and Ed was humbled to be asked to speak. Simply, directly, from his heart, he gave a brief but telling message, the gist of which was, "While all you here today knew this man as a tough ex-Marine, I knew him as a Christian. He is in paradise today."

Don Mott says that people actually walk in off the street and ask him for counsel because they have heard that he is a Christian businessman. His reputation has so spread that he now speaks several times a week, mostly in churches, but also to clubs and other groups, throughout Florida and in many other states.

Walter Barnes is often called on at the bank for invocations and I asked him how it came about. "Well," he said, "you become known by your walk and your talk. Often someone will intimate to me that an off-color conversation has changed to something more wholesome when the group sees me approaching. I don't preach to people in the office, but my Bible at my desk and a chance remark here and there show I'm a Christian. People just naturally come to me with their problems. Even customers pour out their personal problems, and sometimes I am led to say to them, 'Have you ever thought your problem may not be financial, but *spiritual?*'"

An industrialist of my acquaintance who does not consider himself an extrovert says he finds his best opportunities come when people have had some difficult experience. Then there is no need to pursue them. They are looking for aid and comfort, and he finds it easy to tell them Christ is the answer to their difficulties. Many people come to him with no concept of spiritual things, so part of his counseling involves teaching of the value and power of prayer, and a simple outline of what the Bible is.

Tough Assignment?

If all this sounds as though it couldn't quite happen this way, try it and see. To some it may sound too difficult. You may think you can never make yourself obvious as a Christian on the job. (That business about the Bible on the desk, ish!) Think you might be called a fanatic? That might be a good thing!

One day a man came into Don Mott's office to insure his car. "Why did you happen to come to us?" asked Don.

"Well," the man explained, "I'm new in town. I asked the people in my office where to get car insurance and they said, 'Anywhere but Don Mott's agency. They're nothing but a bunch of religious fanatics.' So I came straight to you!" Plenty of other customers feel the same way. Year in and year out, Don leads in sales for the company he represents, American Fire and Casualty.

Why do we Christians so often get the idea right from the start that the world is against us? Maybe Ed Soistman has the answer. In his urging Christians into active witnessing, he has a slogan, "Christianity was never a spectator sport." A picture that goes with the slogan is that of a lion. (Think that over a minute and recall that in ancient Rome, Christians were "participants" while blood-thirsty pagans watched from the stands.)

Suppose you get the courage to take your Bible to the office, and someone sees it and asks, "Hey, can this thing tell ya when the world's comin' to an end?"

Do you panic? Hardly. "Panic is pagan." If need be, just say, "Well, I'm not that familiar with it yet, but I'll do some research and see if I can get you an answer."

Is this retreat or defeat? No, you've already shown that you have five valuable resources:

1. A Bible.
2. Enough interest in it to keep it handy.
3. Therefore, apparently some connection with God.
4. Honesty (by admitting you don't have all the answers).
5. Concern for the questioner (by offering to find his answer.).

That's probably a lot more than anyone else has ever shown for Christ around there, and you may be surprised at where it can lead. Small as it seems, you've taken a step forward.

9

"A Merry Heart Doeth Good"

Nobody likes a sourpuss. The world is so full of gloom and fear that we are all searching for faces that smile and voices that laugh. Though many of us have enough "happiness" to keep up the struggle of life, we don't have enough joy to generate light on our faces. So a person taking a picture always has to remind us to smile.

If you're going to succeed in business while being guided by Christian principles, one of the "Be Attitudes" that will be most helpful is be cheerful, and, if you are equipped for it, even be funny.

Some people who are as happy as can be, well-adjusted, useful, and effective are serious-minded. They do not know how to make fun of their own faults, tell a joke, kid somebody out of a spell of gloom, or use humor in any other way. If you are one of these, you may learn something from this chapter. And you may not. Some experts say humor can be taught. Others disagree. But most people do have at least a small spark of humor, and it can be used to great advantage by the

Christian in business.

We must learn to take our work and our mission in life seriously, but not take *ourselves* too seriously. Proverbs 17:22 says, "A merry heart doeth good like a medicine, but a broken spirit drieth the bones." The world today is sick, and we need a lot of this merry medicine. If you appear to have it, people are going to come to you with their various sicknesses—anger, grief, frustration, confusion, jealousy—and this will give you a natural opening to help heal the sickness in your company.

How will they know that you have the medicine? By the doctor's shingle you have out front—your face. Proverbs 15:13 says, "A merry heart maketh a cheerful countenance, but by sorrow of the heart the spirit is broken."

Some say, "With the mess the world is in, how can I be happy?" If you are truly a Christian you will have a certain joy, regardless of anything that happens to you or anyone else. Tragedy may come, but Christ in us can overcome it. If we have lost all our *own* happiness, there is still hope for the happiness of others. We are to turn our eyes and our efforts away from our own misery and do what we can to relieve the misery of others. And there is an endless supply of it to work on!

But you can't help anyone if you have the biggest frown in town, look like a sufferer from acid indigestion, or a contestant for Mr. Quinceface. Christian virtues magnify enjoyment of life; they don't destroy it. Jesus reminds us, "Moreover when ye fast, be not, as the hypocrites, of a sad countenance: for they disfigure their faces, that they may appear unto men to fast. Verily I say unto you, 'They have their reward'" (Matt. 6:16).

In other words, you don't show your great goodness and piety by being down in the mouth and down on everybody around you, regardless of how evil you think they are. Remember, you're still a sinner too—one of the blessed ones, it's true, because somebody told you about Christ and gave you the opportunity of being saved—but you're still a sinner. "For I say," says Paul, "through the grace given unto me, to every man that is among you, not to think of himself more highly than he ought to think; but to think soberly, according as God hath dealt to every man the measure of faith" (Rom. 12:3).

Break the Ice

You don't have to downgrade yourself, or ever lose your self-respect or deny Christ. But one of the best ways to "break the ice," to get next to people so you can begin spreading the Word, is to use humor. It can take many forms. Because of my funny name, I have learned to use humor in many situations. With a name like Bump, you automatically start a laugh riot when you're introduced, so it's pretty hard to take yourself too seriously. But you don't need a funny name to put humor to work for you.

A pastor I know likes to tell about the time he went into an office and gave the receptionist his name without using the title of Reverend. When she asked if he were a salesman, he smiled and replied, "Well, you might say I'm an insurance salesman. I guess you could say I sell *fire* insurance."

Don Mott, who really is an insurance salesman, used to write a newspaper column as an advertisement for his business. In it he made many a point by a simple, homespun expression or anecdote. One was about a farmer who called Don the "humblest rich man I ever met." Don went on to explain immediately that he did not consider himself rich then or now, but that we are all richer than we think. He further illustrated his humble beginnings by reminiscing about the fact that he was 11 years old before he tasted iced tea. Up to that time he thought it was a rich person's drink. This type of frank and easy revelation that you are not some exalted person and are able to laugh at yourself readily gets people on your side.

What do you do when you're caught in a group in which inappropriate stories are being exchanged? I have excused myself graciously, yet with humor, by remarking as I departed, "If I'm caught listening to one more like that, I'll get kicked out of the Baptist church!" The gang would laugh, but would respect me for standing by my principles.

Save the Situation

I actually helped prevent a most embarrassing and potentially hazardous confrontation in this manner one time. Two men at a company dinner party in a restaurant had drunk too much. Careless words led to real insults, and fists were about to fly. I prayed for what I should do or say to break the tension in the air, to get the two angry men to abandon their quarrel and sit down. Several whispered admonitions to them from others had no effect. I knew my usual cry of being a Baptist would do no good, for what was needed here was a united front of several people to show the pettiness of the impending fight and thus dissolve it by group disapproval. Glancing around the room, I got my answer. There were two couples who belonged to the Latter Day Saints. Taking my wife by the hand and standing up, I said loudly, "All Baptists and Mormons out!"

The party exploded in a roar of laughter that even the would-be fighters couldn't resist. They limply walked back to their tables and peace was resumed.

Admit You Are Human

You can use what I call *comparative* humor to subtly give a message with a moral. Some people who drink, for example, would really rather not, but they don't know how to get out of it. In explaining why you don't drink, you can make it plain that you are not looking down on people who do. You have probably heard the expression, "I'll drink to that!" Well, I invented my own expression, "I'll *eat* to that!" It always gets a laugh, but it also gets the message across: "This guy Bump doesn't need to drink. He has as much fun as anybody."

Point out your own foibles or idiosyncrasies that aren't sin but can be laughed at. Do you have a golf widow in the summer or a TV widow during football season? You don't want to drink, so you say, "No, thanks. My vice is golf (or fishing, bowling, chess, drag racing, dirt-biking, or whatever.)" It'll show that you do not claim to be a plaster saint and are therefore not looking down your nose at anybody, but that at least you cleave to the more innocent pleasures that have less harmful consequences than drunken driving, carousing, and the like. You don't say this in so many words; it is merely implied.

Still another tack some find helpful is to suggest the consequences of sin humorously. As Lucy, in the delightful comic strip "Peanuts," tells Charlie Brown, "The wages of sin is Aaaaaaaarrrgh!"

A witty southern salesman one time told me that it wasn't his inborn honesty that kept him from cheating on his income tax. It was just, as he put it, that "Atlanta is a mighty grim place!" (He was referring to the high, grey walls of the federal penitentiary there.)

Walter Barnes uses this direct approach when he hears someone use the phrase, "Go to hell."

He will chuckle and say, "Are you sure that's what you want for that person? You know hell is quite an awful place. Do you really know how bad it is?"

This will usually bring a sheepish laugh, and quite often Walter finds it easy to follow up with a Bible reference or quotation to get the person thinking more seriously about the subject. Sometimes it has led to a conversation about the need for a person to accept Christ in order to make sure he escapes eternity in hell.

Ed Soistman finds humor a great opener in his talks to various groups. He may begin his talk by revealing that he has a "Ph.D." which he explains means Plain High School Diploma! In what he calls his "key" talk he shows an old skate key which symbolizes his 16 boyhood years in Baltimore when the family was on relief and he had no bike, but did have roller skates. What he finally gets around to is that as he needed the key to skate, we all need a key to live. This, he finally shows, is the Bible.

Reasons to Rejoice

To keep a merry heart, we must constantly cultivate the inner happiness available to us. "Count your blessings" is old advice, but still solid! We do this by thinking how much better off we are than other people, not in a proud way but a happy way, just thanking God for good things we enjoy—and for the bad things that have not happened to us. Think of health, home, country, occupation, possessions. Inadequate though they may be, they're better than someone else has. Look ahead or back to the joys of Christmas, birthday, vacation. Childlike? Maybe, but the Bible tells us to humble ourselves like a little child (Matt. 18:3-4).

In short, your inner happiness begins with mental and spiritual attitude. One of the aids to maintaining it is recreation. All work and no play not only makes Jack a dull boy but a sad one. Recreation relieves tensions. And what is recreation? It's change! Even powerful, vibrant top executives who never take vacations constantly enjoy the recreation of change—traveling, encountering new people, and starting new projects. For them this is fun! People whose work is mostly mental often like to do something physical for recreation, and vice versa. However, you know what you like for recreation. Do it, occasionally. It helps keep you happy.

Another aid to inner happiness is helping others. You find your life by losing it in service, just as Jesus taught us (see Matt. 16:25).

With your basic happiness well established and constantly maintained, it will be easier for you to employ various devices of humor with which to show another person that you have a merry heart and to help him have one also.

When Things Look Grim

A French proverb says, "I laugh because I dare not cry." This means simply looking the Grim Reaper in the face and saying, "Get lost, crumb!" It's whistling in the dark. It's "Hit me again; I'm still conscious." It's "I'm completely surrounded by the enemy. I won't let one of 'em get away!" It's

"What do you mean, use an old ball over the water hazard? I've never *owned* an old ball."

A man being transferred to a distant and undesirable outpost grinned and said, "This is not good-bye. This is the end of everything!"

A chairman of the board, facing stockholders with a depressing, glum, simply awful year-end report, smiles weakly and says, "This is a year we stored up memories."

An aid to maintaining the sense of humor in hopeless situations is the "Look ahead and then look back and laugh" technique. Today you laugh about perilous times through which you passed some time ago. So why not realize that some day you can laugh about this current mess? If some day, then why not now? You will no doubt survive this cataclysm as you have others. So enjoy your laugh now instead of waiting. If you do not survive, at least you will have gone down laughing, like the Kurdish thief: his legend illustrates the sense of humor and the intense love of colors which are characteristics of the inhabitants of Kurdistan. These mid-eastern people mix colors in wild profusion in their clothing. A thief was sentenced to be hanged. Allowed a final request, he thought a minute, then smiled brightly, and said, "Hang me with a red and green rope!"

Besides your basic, built-in happiness and sense of well-being because you are a Christian, there is another aid to being able to laugh, jest, grin, or at least smile feebly during times of trouble. It is the ancient Chinese philosophy: "What will it matter 100 years from now?"

Look up at the stars and realize that the light from them has been on its way to you for thousands, perhaps millions of years. They are so far away you could not reach one in your lifetime, even traveling at the speed of light—186,000 miles per second. Then realize further that beyond the stars you can see, there are other universes full of stars you cannot see. Pretty soon you begin to realize that you are nothing but a speck in time and space. That sort of puts your present li'l ol' problem in perspective, doesn't it?

Up off the canvas, Champ, and start slugging again. You may not be much, but you're all you've got. Maybe nobody appreciates you, but God loves you. Yep. Same God that made all those stars made *you,* and put you here for a reason. Your job: Find the reason. The search takes the form of a game. It's called the Game of Life. Is it fun? Man, it's a riot! Someone has said that the reason it's so tricky is that they keep changing the rules on you. Well, you do have to be flexible, or perhaps a better word is versatile . . . and that's our next subject.

10

How to Represent Christ

A fellow once told me that before becoming a Christian he had been bored to death, but that now he found such daily excitement that he felt as though he were hanging onto a comet and being swished through the sky to some different destination each day. Whether or not it makes you quite that breathless, the Christian life can indeed be exciting at times, and the more you work at it the more exciting it seems to be.

Most of us who try to follow in Christ's giant footsteps have found that one has to be ready for just about anything at any time. This is certainly true if you're going to succeed in business. With God's guidance you can generally map out a long-range plan that will be practical in terms of your immediate preparation. But you will probably find that each day brings a variety of surprises and the need for many adjustments in your plans and methods. "Boast not thyself of tomorrow for thou knowest not what a day may bring forth" (Prov. 27:1). However, "In all thy ways acknowledge

Him, and He shall direct thy paths" (Prov. 3:6).

In walking the Christian way in business you may find yourself mostly alone at first. There may be plenty of other Christians around, but of the timid variety who aren't mentioning anything about their beliefs. You see all the churches in town on the one hand and all the pagan living in the offices, factories, and stores on the other, and you kind of wonder who belongs to all the churches.

The Silencers

The main reason so many Christians are quiet is apparently fear. They may be afraid of being called hypocrites if they ever reveal their beliefs; but they are probably more afraid they will be fired if they fail to conform to practices with which they disagree.

Another reason Christians are afraid is that they might have tried at one time to witness and were repelled because they came on too strongly. Their timing was poor or their approach was too brash. They were unpleasant, "holier-than-thou," or preachy, or even a nuisance. They were taking too much company time in trying to convert someone, or everlastingly showering people with tracts and books they were not the least bit interested in.

They were not "wise as serpents and harmless as doves." They intruded when and where they were not welcome. Christians have told me in some places, "There's no use to talk religion here. Nobody will listen." Well, maybe that was their problem. They *talked "religion"* instead of *living Christianity.*

Opening the Doors

As Ed Soistman so well put it, "You have to begin

by being an example of what Christian living is. It has to rub off from you to others. One day some guys got to discussing what rotten shape the world was in and wondering aloud how much longer things could go on getting worse all the time. 'Yeah,' I said, 'if I didn't know that God planned one Flood, I think if I saw an old guy out somewhere building a big boat, I'd start helping him.'"

Ed also makes his own openings to Christian conversations by using an idea he got from the company. It was the policy to send birthday cards, so he now has his own birthday cards he sends to the people in his department. He puts something special in each card—a personal note or perhaps a tract. He has found that his greeting is the only birthday card some people receive! He has found that another method of getting close enough to people to break down their barriers of shyness about conversing on spiritual matters is to make sure he tells them everything he can about the company, its work, and their jobs. In other words, he tries to have as much communication as possible. He finds it builds trust.

Attending the weekly 6:30 A.M. Friday prayer breakfast of the Winter Park Christian Business Men's Committee brings him to the office about an hour later than his usual 7 A.M. arrival time. When the plant entrance guards became curious as to this regular pattern, he saw an opportunity to witness merely by telling where he went on Fridays. This led to questions about the group, and the guards gained a firm understanding and friendly respect for this key executive's Christian stand. After that, just seeing him come in was a weekly reminder to them that he valued prayer and fellowship with other Christians.

Jim Burnett uses the simple device of a sign in his store to get people to discussing spiritual things. The sign says, "Christ is the Lord of *humanity* and not *profanity*." He got the idea for it when he became a Christian and began to conquer his own bad profanity habit. Jim has also found that merely being sociable when he has repaired someone's refrigerator on a service call can open the conversation to spiritual things. "I used to just do the job and get out of the house or business as quickly as I could," he says. "But now I try to keep alert for any sign that the person seems troubled over something more than an electrical appliance problem. Being as friendly and pleasant as possible sometimes opens the way for comments or questions from a customer that show me how I can witness to this person."

A representative of Amana, a major appliance maker, became a Christian due to Jim's influence. Giving his testimony before a group, he explained, "I was inspired by things at Burnett's." The representative changed his dealer meetings from cocktail parties to luncheons. It affected 50 dealers in the Central Florida area alone—affected them well, for their business increased.

Wear Christ's Badge

Prayer, thought, and imagination will lead you to right ways of handling yourself in various situations and with various kinds of persons. At first you must be patient. You cannot burst into a business and start a revival the first day and probably not even the first month. You can, however, make it clear from your life, and from the most matter-of-fact conversation, that you are a Christian.

Clarence Trowbridge, a factory worker, writing in *Moody Monthly*, ("Dilemma in the Factory,"

August 1957) says, "Your fellow employees must understand that you are a Christian before you try to live like a Christian. If you fail to do this your good behavior will be put down either as spitefulness or just plain orneriness by the other workers.

"I am not saying that a man cannot be a Christian without making an open issue of it. Indeed, I think that the majority of Christians are trying to do just exactly that. I have seen many of these 'secret' Christians.

"I will say that any attempt to live the Christian life in a crowded factory will end in defeat and heartache if the Christian will not take a stand for Christ. The temptations will come at the secret Christian so thick and fast that his head will fairly spin.

"By making a stand and sticking to it, the Christian automatically short-circuits many temptations. Once the unsaved men understand your position they will often decide for themselves that a thing is wrong for you and never even present it to you for a decision."

I found this true. The invitations to cocktail parties, to join betting pools, to listen to off-color stories became fewer and fewer as more and more people got to know my stand. I also found true the principles Trowbridge mentions here:

"Again, if you leave the room when the language becomes too sickening, they will look at one another and nod—but they'll understand.

"When you bow your head over your lunch bucket the men will know what you are doing, and only the meanest will try to bother you. In fact . . . he may find . . . that he has incurred the disapproval of the men. For even the most black-hearted sense that there is something wrong in disturbing a man who is talking to God.

"If your stand is open enough you may find that it becomes almost unnecessary to 'preach the Gospel.' You will become an "epistle, known and read of all men.'

"Moreover, you will find the unsaved coming to you. They will often seek you out whenever they think they can have a word with you in private. At first their questions may concern factual things like ethics and Bible truths. It is their way of finding out whether or not you will be able to answer their questions.

"Later, when their confidence in you has increased, they will come out with the real question that has been troubling them. If ever a Christian has a God-given chance to testify for Christ, it is at that time."

Be Yourself

So take your opportunities as they come, at the pace you feel is right for you. Some Christians work fast. Some slowly. Some are dynamic. Some are quiet. "Now there are diversities of gifts, but the same Spirit. And there are differences of administrations, but the same Lord. And there are diversities of operations, but it is the same God which worketh all in all" (1 Cor. 12:4-6).

You are an individual with as good a potential as Peter, Paul, and the rest—probably *better*, because of today's mass communications. We are the best-read, most well-informed generation in history. With television bringing actual scenes of current battles, political events, daily developments in medicine, education, labor, and economics right into our homes; with newspapers, magazines, and books filling in details for us as never before, we are the best equipped people of all time to spread the Gospel by showing how we use it to respond to the onrush of life.

Have no fear about what you are going to do or say. God will use you to the utmost as you let yourself be used! He will show you what to do with what you are and what you have, right where you are, just as He did those tough, smelly, salty-tongued fishermen, Peter, Andrew, and the others, and that scheming religious fanatic, Saul of Tarsus, whose name later became Paul.

"Now ye are the body of Christ, and members in particular. And God hath set some in the church, first apostles, secondarily prophets, thirdly teachers, after that miracles, then gifts of healings, helps, governments, diversities of tongues. Are all apostles? Are all prophets? Are all teachers? Are all workers of miracles? Have all the gifts of healing? Do all speak with tongues? Do all interpret? But covet earnestly the best gifts" (1 Cor. 12:27-31).

Try Different Tactics

You may have tried and not accomplished much (though you may have touched some nerves that you know nothing about). You may be so low on the totem pole that you know no one is listening. You may find that, as some comedian put it, "I make so little impression that when I enter a room it's like someone just left!"

Here again, you need to be versatile. You need to be ready to change tactics. You may be a better follower than a leader, and believe me, leaders need followers, else whom would the leaders lead? So whom do you follow?

The early Christians formed what they called cells, groups of from two to a dozen. As they grew they would divide and form a new cell, just as nature's cells do in the body. All it takes to start a cell is you and one other person. If you can discover or win one other Christian besides yourself, you have the beginning of a cell. You don't have to have regular meetings or make regular plans or do anything formal; just keep in touch with one another and share your prayers, experiences, and problems, plans, ideas, victories, and defeats in any scraps of time you can find that are *your own!* (Don't steal company time. That's like stealing money.)

Your conversations with your cell members do not always have to be on the subject of how to evangelize the company. Take a wide general interest in each other, so you can give comfort in family problems and share enthusiasm about hobbies or other interests. The more you get to know and support each other, the better will be your work as a Christian team. You will gain courage and inspiration from each other.

Another advantage of the cell plan is that, without making any fearful efforts to reach out to someone you feel you should win, you may find that person attracted to your group. He or she may have wanted to speak to you about your Christian stand, but did not have the courage until finding there was another person or two "like you," standing with you. Timid Christians may also surface as a result of your cell. I saw this happen many times.

Seek Help
If you need help in "getting something started" where you work, you can find it through groups like the Christian Business Men's or Christian

Business Women's Committees, or some other lay-men's organization. If no such group exists, talk to your pastor or some Christian business or profes-sional person in your church or in some other church or in your service club or lodge. There are people in all walks of life who have found ways to take a Christian stand in their work. They are willing to share what they have done and what they have heard of others doing. Ask enough questions long enough, and you'll find the key.

You may find that the best strategy is to form a group of sympathetic and helpful Christians away from where you work. Have regular meetings such as luncheons, breakfasts, or whatever format fits best for prayer, Bible study, and the creation and sharing of Christian strategy that will help you where you work.

This, of course, is basically what a church does, but because business crosses denominational lines, Christian business and professional groups have been organized outside of churches. Another reason, of course, is that the very mention of "church" scares away some people. They will risk attending a businessmen's lunch, even if they know some "religion" may be mentioned, as long as you don't tag the group with the name of some church. (Some fear they may be asked to join your denomination; some feel that the church—any church—is a dead institution; some think that to be a church member you have to pay "dues"; and some declare that the only place to worship is the wide open spaces.)

I was won to Christ by an attorney with whom I was having lunch in a drugstore. I was already a devout church worker in a major Protestant de-nomination, and not antagonistic to the Gospel in any way. I believed in God as the Creator and

Controller of the universe, in Jesus as His Son, and I prayed and studied the Bible some. But no one had ever clearly brought me face to face with my need to accept Christ as personal Saviour.

All those people out there aren't really against Christ. Some are just as I was, not really *for* Him. Your job may be a lot easier than you think. All you may have to do for some folks is clearly explain the plan of salvation as the attorney did for me.

But you may have to use some imagination, some ingenuity. This attorney was in a movement whose people were doing just as Christ did, going about reaching others on a person-to-person basis. They confronted them with the Man Jesus Christ, the Son of God, born of a virgin, performing miracles, crucified, buried, risen and coming again—all for the sake of saving sinners. Take Him or leave Him. Take Him, and your place in heaven with God for eternity is secure. Leave Him, and you are condemned to burn for eternity in hell.

They added only a basic plan for helping you live a Christian life after you accepted Him—have a "quiet time" of Bible study, listening, and prayer, with a notebook to write down your guidance for the day; make resitution to the people you have wronged; pray for people you hate; follow the Golden Rule; and continue to serve Christ in whatever denomination you are already in.

The way the whole thing was put was as much a challenge as an invitation. Somehow the simple story of Christ's love and sacrifice had never been presented to me as clearly. Christ died that I might have life. All I had to do was accept. Why hadn't someone said so before? I was 21 years old. I accepted. Your work may be as easy as the attorney's was in winning me to the Lord. Sometimes all we need to do is get someone to sit still long enough to tell them the Story!

Don't Overlook the Church

But suppose you have no prospects of organizing a cell where you work or a Christian business group outside. You are not an organizer, an administrative type, or a social animal at all. Yet you want some of those around you to at least hear the Story. You can't tell them yourself, somehow. What do you do? If you can say three words, you can do something that may be enough. The words are "Come to church."

You don't have to put any pressure behind the words or add any salesmanship about Christianity or your denomination or your congregation or anything else. All you have to do is give a courteous invitation and the time of the services. Naturally the invitation is made easier if there is something special going on such as a revival, a film, or a supper, but you do not need to wait for anything like that. A simple invitation to a regular worship service or to Sunday School may get the person there. Do you realize that there are people who have never been to church simply because they haven't been invited? Do you realize that some folks were once active in church but drifted away and never got back, simply because no one ever asked them to try it again? And there are those who are timid and actually feel that they are *unworthy* to attend church. ("The roof would fall if I ever walked in!" Remember?)

Don't be surprised if nobody accepts your invitation. As pointed out before, there are people who won't go to church ever—unless their funeral happens to be conducted there. But, on the other hand, don't be surprised, either, if someone does accept your invitation. And don't be surprised at another strange result that may come from your simple act of inviting someone to church: you may find, as I did, that this mere mention of church can be the beginning of opening your mouth to real witnessing.

Everyone has to start somewhere, if he starts at all, and that is where I started. I, too, was once tongue-tied as far as Christian witnessing on the job. It was the simple act of inviting someone to church that got me started on the road to talking about deeper things than just "church." After I had been able to get that much out without unpleasant aftereffects, I was encouraged to mention some things that went on at church—a joke the preacher told, a cute thing some little kid did in the Vacation Bible School program or an experience some man had shared in a Sunday School class. Little by little I found that I was talking more freely of my beliefs and my Christian experience.

And then people began to come to me with questions and problems. At that point the way is open to you to really witness and counsel, for all you have to do is answer their questions. This leads to making suggestions and giving them ideas, and quoting Scripture to show where the ideas came from or to give evidence of their validity. By then, the people who come to you are not only willing to listen, but eager, because they see in you a source of real help. You do your part—no matter how small—in any way God shows you, and He will do the rest. Whether you're just a "hey-you" or the top banana where you work, you can succeed. The word will get around.

11

The Word Will Get Around

One of the things God will do if you serve Him where you are is give you a little prominence. It may not be the kind you like, but you are going to become known. You are going to make an impression. When you start to brighten the corner where you are, people are going to see your little light and say:

"Hey, what's that?" "Who does he think he is, anyway?" "Hmmm. That cat seems to have something I'd like to have."

The next thing you know, somebody overhears such a comment and this attracts even more attention. There's something "different" about you, because practicing Christians today are all too scarce.

You're going to be noticed just as Acts 4:13 tells us that Peter and John were: "Now when they saw the boldness of Peter and John, and perceived that they were unlearned and ignorant men, they marveled; and they took knowledge of them, that they had been with Jesus." You may not be bold. You may be scared to death, but you've been with

Jesus, in fact, *are* with Him; and it shows!

Every Christian businessman I talk to has had a similar experience. They say that when they live Christ on the job, people notice it and react, just as they reacted to Him when He was on earth— some for, some against.

We all like recognition; *need* it, in fact. It's one of the basic psychological or sociological needs. We prefer the pleasant, favorable kind; but if we can't get that, we'll take the unfavorable kind. Do anything to us except ignore us. Now you don't become a Christian in order to get recognition. It comes as a by-product.

You'll get *favorable* recognition from three sources: Those who know what you are and who want what you have; those whom you help; and those who don't know what makes you tick but see you as an asset to the company.

I enjoyed many laughs at being called "Bump, the Baptist," and appreciated the confidence people placed in me because they felt I had "connections" with God.

I'll never forget the time a man who owned a boat rental and fish-bait business asked me to pray for rain. A long dry spell had just about dried up the lake and his business. He thought he had to operate on Sunday mornings and I was trying to talk him out of it, but I promised to pray for rain so his business would be so good during the week he could close on Sunday mornings. I prayed for rain, but there must have been an awful lot of others praying too, for we got not only a rain but a flood! The town was paralyzed. Some people were evacuated from their homes. The Red Cross came. It was a lulu!

When the sun came out again and the lake went

down enough for the boat and bait man to collect his scattered little fleet and his worms and minnows, I went back to see him. "Man!" he said, "when you pray you don't kid around, do you!" As far as I know he never did close on Sundays, but the Lord closed him for one Sunday anyhow.

For a long time after that when an outing was being planned by my company, often someone would say, "Can you get us any help on making sure we have good weather?"

"Known and Read of All Men"

The industrial executive I mentioned earlier said he became known right away as a Christian, due to his refusal to drink. People respected him for it, and as they came to realize other aspects of his Christian stand, their respect grew. "I've never been persecuted," he grinned, "but maybe that shows I'm not living as strong a Christian life as I should."

Well, do any of us? Probably not. I think if every man served Christ in business as well as that executive, however, the business world would be a much more wholesome place.

Barnes, the banker, has been kidded about being a local "Billy Graham" but he kids right back, pointing out that he gets no more excited about Christianity than some folks do about football or golf. He is well-liked and has the confidence of the people who know him.

Trovillion, the contractor, became so well known as a Christian businessman he was elected mayor. During his years in office he was approached by only one person who knew his reputation so little that he tried to interest the mayor in a shady deal.

Soistman, the aerospace executive, said he had a fortunate start in his company because his boss was G. T. Willey, an active and well-known Christian businessman who was then vice president and general manager. They were able to work as a leadership team, opening business programs with prayer and letting fellow executives in conferences know that the staff meeting was no place for profanity. Visitors also soon began to sense in the plant an esprit de corps and code of ethics higher than in many comparable companies they contacted. The example rubbed off onto them and they spread it to other states.

Negative Reactions

You may find, however, when you announce your stand or are revealed by your conduct as a Christian, that you will not be favorably received. Scripture warns, "Yea, and all that will live godly in Christ Jesus shall suffer persecution" (2 Tim. 3:12). As the favorable reactions come to you largely from three groups, the unfavorable ones will come from four others: those who know and want what you have but won't admit it; those whom you haven't helped; those who consider you a fanatic, nut, menace, or nuisance; and those who are envious of your happiness but too weak, afraid, or proud to try to claim it for themselves.

Though the people who oppose, ridicule or ignore you may inflict on you a kind of persecution, may try to make life miserable, prevent your getting promotions, or even get you fired, you have nothing to fear from them.

"Nothing to fear?" you scream. "Getting fired is nothing? Easy for you to say!"

Well, as we saw in chapter 3, loss of a job does

not mean loss of life or hope. But what if you keep your job and are tormented? What kind of reward is this? Naturally, if it gets worse instead of better and goes on and on, you don't need to stay forever and take it. "Give not that which is holy unto the dogs, neither cast ye your pearls before swine, lest they trample them under their feet, and turn again and rend you" (Matt. 7:6). "And whosoever shall not receive you, nor hear your words, when ye depart out of that house or city, shake off the dust of your feet" (Matt. 10:14).

But don't be too quick to quit. Give the place a fair test. Give yourself and the Lord some time to see whether you can make it here, unless, of course, He tells you immediately to leave. Some persons don't make friends quickly at best. The additional quality that you have—your Christian stand—can be an extra barrier. Some of your somewhat aloof co-workers are not scornful. They're just naturally shy, even timid. Some of them are puzzled by you. They've never seen a real, live Christian in captivity before; only read about them or heard about them in sermons. It is best, they think, to observe a while before going on record as being a friend or prospective friend.

Play it just as cool as the fearful one for a while. Be friendly, but don't give with the big, waggly, hairy puppy approach yet. No need to pursue those who give you the great stone face, but don't brood over their attitude. People whom I thought I could never approach about Christ have come to me after months, even years, of "looking me over." They just had to decide in their own good time that I was not some high priest of hypocrisy, but was one of the human race, an ordinary joe who had found something quite extraordinary to hang on to.

You may be surprised, too, after some months, to find that some of the persons who have held you at a distance are Christians! Receiving Christ does not automatically make one an eager extrovert who extends the glad hand of hearty welcome to new-comers. Some Christians are quiet, shy people, always were and always will be. God made all kinds of folks—loud, soft, and medium. Some of us change through education, training, and experience, and some do not. The chances are that the Christian who is a natural introvert will remain basically that way because he lives honestly and does not try to put on a front. He may overcome any shyness that is an actual handicap because Christ does help us improve our personalities, but basically the introvert is a quiet person—and aren't we glad there are some quiet ones in this noisy world? It may take quite a while to get acquainted with a person like this. You will learn, to your amazement, that he or she was not hostile but just marking time to the quiet clock inside that would eventually bring the hour of opportunity for saying, "Say, I've been meaning to ask you . . ."

A reticent Christian may not be an introvert at all, however. He may be as outgoing as anyone, but wary of an active, witnessing Christian like yourself because he has been unable or unwilling to take the stand you have taken in the work place. He may actually be eager to get with you and thank you for "coming to the rescue" or "giving me courage," but he may hang back for some time, waiting to see how you "turn out"—whether your obviousness as a Christian makes or loses friends for you, gets you promoted or terminated. Or, he may be one of the Christians we mentioned earlier who has tried in the wrong way to witness, and,

having failed, does not want to openly ally himself
with you because he feels *you* will fail, too.

Controversial Beats Unknown

Let's say you've sized up the situation and decided
that though you are not instantly the most popular
person around, you will not be completely ostra-
cized. You decide to stick around a while and see
what happens. One thing sure, you have made an
impression, an image. It may change some in the
eyes of various ones, as their knowledge of you
grows. But, good or bad, your start has been made.
You have to have some kind of image in order to
be useful to Christ's cause. You may not be a "real
somebody" yet, but at least you're not a "nobody."
You are probably at this point a controversial
figure. Some are for you, some against.

You have to be known or at least "known of"
before you can be recognized. This is not only a
requirement for Christian service, but for succeeding in business, so taking your Christian stand has
done two things for you already. It has given you
identity as a Christian and as a person—maybe only
"the new kid on the block" but at least a member
of the team. Nobody may know much about you,
but they know you're here. Your image will either
help you stay, rise higher here, or take you elsewhere in His service.

Jim Burnett says that air-conditioning and refrigeration customers come to him saying, "We've been
referred to you as a man of exceptional character.
We could get this job done cheaper, but we want
to do business with you."

Thus Jim may find himself witnessing in a grocery
store, a motor repair shop, or a restaurant. He never
knows where the Lord will have him speak next,

or where someone will speak to him about the Lord because of having heard that Jim is in partnership with Him and has answers questions about life.

Don Mott's mail bulges more and more with requests to speak. He has given talks from Taft, Florida, to Tokyo, Japan. Groups throughout the South and various parts of the country and the world have heard that he mixes Christianity and business in a most successful manner. This man who sells insurance for life can also tell about *assurance* for the after-life.

Ed Soistman's image has so spread that his hobby is not golf, but speaking to churches and other groups, visiting hospitals and other institutions where people need help.

Walt Meloon's audiences have summoned him to places as far away as New Guinea. Among Correct Craft's customers are King Hussein of Jordan and the Shah of Iran.

Yes, the word will get around, when you start making it known that you are one who likes to get the Word around, one who dares call himself a Christian, a "churchman," somebody "religious." You may be kidded as being a company "chaplain," but the very ones who call you that may later come for help.

You Won't Always Win

What of the others—those who never do warm up to you, those who shun you because of your Christian stand? "Blessed are ye when men shall say all manner of evil against you falsely, for My sake" (Matt. 5:11). "And they departed from the presence of the council, rejoicing that they were counted worthy to suffer shame for His name" (Acts 5:41).

The word will get around all right. Sooner or later, here or elsewhere, you'll become known for what you are.

You may not see any tangible evidence that being a Christian helps you succeed. Some Christians actually feel it is a hindrance to climbing as high on the money ladder as might otherwise have been possible.

What kind of success does God want you to have? At the end of Walt Disney's film biography, he says that one of his brothers who was a mailman had as much success as he. As Walt put it, "He was the one who had all the fun." All he had to do was deliver the mail and then he could go fishing or whatever he wanted to do, whereas Walt felt his life had always been tied up in story conferences, or working with artists, bankers, lawyers, and all that.

If you serve the Lord in business as you do at home or anywhere else, He will help you conquer obstacles and find success, the kind He wants you to have.

12

Everybody Wins

You have made a beginning. You have either started on a job or in your own business determined to hold to Christian principles. Perhaps you have begun boldly, perhaps timidly, but at least you have begun. You don't know how it's going to turn out; whether you'll be able to keep it up; and, if you do keep it up, what effect it will have on your future. Will your employer and fellow employees continue to accept you? Will your customers continue to do business with you?

It is at this point, when such questions arise in the mind, that we separate the men from the boys, the Christian soldiers from the Christian draft-dodgers. Will you hang in there or quit?

Did you take the cold plunge or the quiet, creeping approach to letting people know you are a Christian? The cold plunge method is to make it clear from the first that you are a Christian. The quiet, creeping approach describes what happened to me. As I gradually let Christ get more and more control of my life, people gathered from the things

I was saying and the decisions I was making that I could not live with some commonly accepted practices. After a few such incidents when I plainly took a Christian stand, it became evident to everyone that I was "different." When the questions began, I was strengthened in my witness. I found it easy to explain why I believed as I did.

Winning Over Discouragement

If you have the unusual advantage of going to work for a Christian boss as Ed Soistman or Walt Meloon did, you will find some help in living by Christ's standards. But even then the way is not going to be ginger-peachy. So do not be discouraged if you find yourself discouraged.

How's that again? That's right, nothing is so discouraging as discouragement itself. So don't be discouraged just because you feel discouraged. It's normal, not only among laymen but among pastors. Don't you know that many pastors want to quit every Monday morning? If a man who is a full-time, paid professional Christian can feel like giving up, is it any wonder you, an untrained, inexperienced, frightened, lay person among a bunch of smoking, drinking, swearing heathen should figure, "What's the use?"

But you determined, perhaps at a time when you felt stronger than you do now, that you were going to work the Christian way. So do it, even if it kills you. "No man, having put his hand to the plow, and looking back, is fit for the kingdom of God" (Luke 9:62).

God does not ask miracles of you. That's His department. "But seek ye first the kingdom of God, and His righteousness; and all these things shall be added unto you" (Matt. 6:33). "Ask and it shall be given you; seek and ye shall find; knock and it shall be opened unto you" (Matt. 7:7).

You won't get all the answers and the strength of a Walt Meloon or Don Mott, R. G. LeTourneau or J. C. Penney overnight. They didn't get power that fast either. But just do what God says to do *this* day, this hour, and little by little you'll gain strength and effectiveness without realizing it.

I was surprised and humbled once when a man in our church said to me sincerely in the course of a conversation, "I could never be the great Christian you are, but. . . ."

No! Had I become so pious, prominent, and pompous that he felt I was a step above? I later analyzed his picture of me and decided he had confused my various leadership activities in Sunday School, deacons, finance committee with "great Christianity." But I also remembered that when I began my Christian walk I too looked to church leaders and mature Christian businessmen and said, "If only I could be like them."

Growth Takes Time

If that's what you're thinking, and if you don't see how it can ever be, take heart. Like any other growth—from freshman to senior, from apprentice to master craftsman, from private to colonel, it takes time, desire, and dedication. You may never be what is considered famous. No book may ever be written about you. You may never even know for sure that you have changed the spiritual climate where you work.

Some missionaries say they have served for 30 years and never felt they had changed the people at all. But how can we judge? How can we know what their mission field would have been like if they had not been there? How can you know what your company would have been like without your efforts to live Christ there?

No, you may never know what effect you have had. Or it may be made evident to you years latei The judging and evaluation is not your job. Therefore, don't worry about your seeming lack of prog ress in influencing others, either now or later. You have made one simple vow: to live Christ where you work, without interfering with your work! Do that and you will succeed!

Your success will be counted in many ways:

First, you will succeed on the job! You will have an income with which to support yourself and family, help educate your children, pay taxes, contribute to God's work and community projects.

You do not have to become a great leader in business, medicine, law, education, or the church. Simply living a wholesome, productive Christian life as a loyal worker for your company and citizen of your community is enough. Naturally, if you have special talents, have been gifted with a good education or a lot of "lucky breaks," God says you should use these. "For unto whomsoever much is given, of him shall be much required; and to whom men have committed much, of him they will ask the more" (Luke 12:48). The more you use what you have, the higher you will climb—in business and in Christian effectiveness.

Second, you will be a success because you will have a happier home life. If you succeed in your work, at the same time holding strong as a Christian, you will be a better husband and father, or wife and mother, because you will have had to first arrange for a Christian home life in order to be a Christian on the job.

Third, you will be a success because you are better able to help people in your church. Sharing some of your experience from the business world will give other church members aid in working out their own business problems in a Christian manner.

Fourth, you will be a success because you have learned to help other people with their problems. As mentioned earlier, people on the job are going to come to you for all kinds of advice. You are going to receive a free education in counseling. Most of it is simply "hand-holding"—listening, showing that you understand, and letting the person see his problem more clearly by talking it out.

Finally, you will be a success because you give the company more than your work. You are an effective worker or executive. You are either a loyal part of the "nuts and bolts" operation of the place or a wise leader who knows which button to press to make sure orders come in, production rolls, quality and service are maintained, and the company stays in business and grows. But you are also a help to the company because you have been able to add a little something that not just anyone can give—harmony, cooperation, a spirit of "want to" instead of "have to."

If we had enough Christians in business there would be no strikes, no slowdowns, no sabotage. Efficiency, safety, production, quality, service, wages, salaries, and dividends would rise. Waste, accidents, sicktime, product failure, and costs would drop. One simple evidence of this is in companies which have profit-sharing, suggestion plans, and other means of "getting everybody into the act."

Having all employees share in ownership of the company is a Christian concept, whether management realizes it or not. Any plan which emphasizes the worth of the individual person is, to that extent, a Christian plan.

This, you see, is one reason America grew so rapidly. What the Pilgrims and Puritans wanted to escape was tyranny. They wanted to worship and to govern themselves in a manner in which each person could enjoy freedom to develop his own God-given talents in the best way. Isaiah said it 2,700 years ago, "The spirit of the Lord God is upon me; because the Lord hath anointed me to preach good tidings unto the meek; He hath sent me to bind up the brokenhearted, to proclaim liberty to the captives, and the opening of the prison to them that are bound" (Isa. 61:1). And Jesus quoted this passage in proclaiming His own mission (Luke 4:18).

Brighten Your Corner

This, too, is your mission in business. You can preach good tidings to the meek and bind up the broken-hearted. Just your being there with your happy, optimistic, positive outlook on life and your calm reassurance because of your faith will preach good tidings. No matter how weak or quiet you are, you have a spark of something as a Christian that non-Christians want and need. And as you gain strength to speak and explain what you stand for, this is going to give more good tidings.

You can bind up the brokenhearted by using your best Sunday smile on Monday—and through the week. It may be worth more than you ever know to someone—and it may be worth more than you realize to *you*, too!

You can proclaim liberty to the captives. So many people are captives of their own fear, selfishness, lack of faith, or lack of other Christian principles! Survey after survey has shown that anywhere from a third to half of the people in this country hate their jobs. They either don't like the people they work with, don't enjoy what they do, don't believe it has much value, or feel they are capable of more pleasant, more profitable work. Yet they don't have the courage or the know-how to break out and try for something else, so they stay on year after year feeling enslaved.

Sometimes all it takes to make such people happy in their work is to show them the significance of what they do; to show them that all work is honorable if done for a good product or service. Sometimes all a person needs is to see the people around him from a Christian point of view to realize that they are not such bad people after all. It is this Christian point of view that you can bring to the place you work.

The Power of Prayer

When someone is griping about another person who really is a problem, you can inject a new thought by saying, "Yes, we do need to pray for him." Whenever I did this I observed a noticeable impact. This simple, basic Christian idea of praying for our enemies is so seldom thought of or practiced today that when it's mentioned it seems to come as a completely revolutionary suggestion, and usually brings on a sudden thoughtful silence, followed perhaps by a "Hmmm! Do you think that'll help?"

As a Christian you know it will, if anything can, so you say, "Yes, indeed!"

Another effect this suggestion usually has is to shut off the stream of accusations and other complaints about the problem person. The mention of prayer suddenly reminds the person you're talking to that it's been a long time since he prayed for *anybody*, for any reason, and maybe a long time since he even has thought about anything spiritual. By the mere mention of the possibility of praying for someone else, you have subconsciously started the complaining person thinking along lines of getting the beam from his own eye before he can cast the mote from anybody else's. He may never have heard that particular command of Christ's, but he is already pausing to think that he isn't worthy to pray for anybody; he isn't exactly perfect, either.

The concept of praying for someone leads naturally to the thought of looking a little closer at the person to be prayed for, thinking more about him, and therefore questioning why he is so disliked and why he acts the way he does. This is the beginning of building a bridge of understanding, which in turn can lead to at least a working cooperation if not real friendship.

The Gift of Encouragement

Your Christian outlook may also aid you in helping some disgruntled person who is unhappy on the job because he cannot see its value. The old illustration of the three masons building a wall says it well. One, when asked what he was doing, simply grumbled, "Settin' stone." The second muttered, "Makin' my pay." But the third, taking time to look up at the progress of the work, declared proudly, "I am building a cathedral!" Which are you doing? What about your fellow workers?

Standing at a production line, tightening one bolt on unknown objects going by is not a very inspirational job. But if you know that the plant turns out aircraft parts, you can point out to the bored guy that he's helping executives fly across the country, thus helping keep the wheels of a thousand different businesses turning; helping people visit relatives; and helping provide jobs for pilots, mechanics, stewardesses, baggage handlers, and ticket agents. If it's military aircraft, he's helping defend the country as much as if he were flying one of those jet fighters himself.

Every job has a reason for being and involves a long chain of consequences when you start thinking about it. But some people never do think beyond the workbench, desk, or machine. Simply helping them raise their sights is a Christian action because it gives them more reason for being, a richer view of life. You're also making that person more valuable to the company because an interested employee does better work.

Then there is the person who hates his job because he doesn't have the courage to break out into something else. Show him that God who created the universe and controls it is all-powerful; that if He can give a person a vision of a better deal, He can also give the means to fulfill it. Use faith stories from the Bible, and from your own life, or the lives of others. Try to get the person to see that genius and education are not the sole prerequisites for success, but that dedicated work and faith are the stars that steer us to success in efforts we enjoy and feel are worthy.

Explain that God wants us to be happy, that He wants us to make the most of what we have, that He has placed us in a world of things, and that there is nothing evil about earning, owning, and using things.

Explain that problems are opportunities in disguise, and that each problem contains the seed of its own solution.

You are succeeding in business without abandoning Christ's rules, without becoming a pagan. If people come to you with their problems, share liberally the reason for your happiness and success —your conviction that everybody can win, with Christ. The more you share, the firmer will become your own belief—in God, in Christ, and in yourself. And this will help to bring you what you started after in the first place—more success!